THE MINISTRY OF
Parenting Your Baby

William Sears, M.D. • Martha Sears, R.N.

THE MINISTRY OF
Parenting Your Baby

LIFEJOURNEY
BOOKS

LifeJourney Books is an imprint of David C. Cook Publishing Co.
David C. Cook Publishing Co., Elgin, Illinois 60120
David C. Cook Publishing Co., Weston, Ontario

THE MINISTRY OF PARENTING YOUR BABY
© 1990 William and Martha Sears

Edited by LoraBeth Norton
Cover design by Dawn Lauck
Cover illustration by Terry Julien

Unless otherwise specified, Scripture quotations are from the *Holy Bible: New International
Version* © 1973, 1978, 1984 by International Bible Society. Used by permission of
Zondervan Bible Publishers.

First printing, 1990
Printed in the United States of America
94 93 92 92 90 5 4 3 2 1

Sears, William, M.D.
    The ministry of parenting your baby / William Sears, Martha Sears
        p.   cm.
    ISBN 1-55513-627-3
    1. Parents—Religious life. 2. Infants—Care. 3. Family—Religious life.
    4. Parenting— Religious aspects—Christianity.
    I. Sears, Martha.   II. Title.
    BV4845.S42 1990
    248.8′45—dc20   90-43105
                                                           CIP

To our quiver full:

James

    Robert

        Peter

            Hayden

                Erin

                    Matthew

                        Stephen

"Like arrows in the hands of a warrior are sons born in one's youth. Blessed is the man whose quiver is full of them."
(Psalm 127:4-5)

TABLE OF CONTENTS

PREFACE

Enormous changes in parenting styles have occurred during this century—changes we perceive as a series of disruptions in God's design for the care and feeding of His children.

The first upset in mother-infant attachment began in the early 1900s, when childbirth began to be considered a "disease." Birthing, from the beginning of time an event which took place in the home and belonged to the family, was transferred to the hospital, where mothers were put to sleep in order to be relieved of this disease by the "operation" of birth.

After birth, babies were placed in plastic boxes and cared for according to a convenient schedule by "experts" in baby care who had no biological attachment to their charges. Father, being regarded as inept and unclean, was banished from the delivery room and could only observe his baby through a glass window. Meanwhile, mother recovered from her "operation" in a separate room. At the very time in a new mother's life when her body was most biologically programmed to care for her baby, she was not encouraged to do so. The pair got off to the wrong start.

Bottle feeding became the next break in God's design for parenting. Taking their cue from the obstetrical practices of detachment, specialists in the care and feeding of babies preached the use of commercial formula, convincing mothers that commercial formula was as good (or better!)—and a lot easier to provide—than their own milk. Mothers allowed themselves to succumb to these marketing practices, and by 1950 breastfeeding in this country had declined to a pitiful twenty percent. And not only were fewer infants receiving the nutrition that God had designed for them, but those women who did dare to breastfeed yielded to peer pressure to wean early.

The next blow to God's design for mother-infant attachment was the term "schedule." If bottle feeding allowed mothers to schedule the baby's tummy, why not schedule the whole baby? "Don't get tied down" was the message of those prophets of bad baby advice. Coincident with these changing parenting styles came the economic constraints of World War II in which many mothers, of necessity, left their homes to enter the world of work.

In the fifties, four-bedroom-house affluence and the general detachment style of parenting led child rearing advisors to proclaim, "Don't let your baby in your bed." Another blow to mother-baby attachment. Now the baby was separated from mother at birth, separated from mother's breast, separated by day, and separated by night. The natural harmony between mother and child was disrupted. Parents did not know their child, since their own intuition had been watered down by this detachment philosophy. The child did not feel right, therefore did not act right, and therefore was less of a joy to the parent. Children began exhibiting undesirable behaviors which were so common as to be later defined as "normal."

Our society has a marvelous way of creating a disease and then coming up with the medicine for that disease. The medicine for this disease of undesirable behavior in children came to us in the fifties in the form of baby books. Schools of child psychology sprang up to rescue parents who no longer knew how to train up their children. Discipline became a science of methods from without, rather than a feeling from within.

These baby books violated one basic rule of parenting—difficult problems in child rearing do not have easy answers. But parents wanted easy answers. For example: "Doctor what do I do when my baby wakes up crying at night?" Answer, "Let your baby cry one hour the first night, forty-five minutes the next night, half an hour the next, and by the fourth night he'll sleep through."

Doctors advised in generalities, and mothers began to think in generalities. This was the era of check-list parenting, of calendar parenting, and of schedules. As parents lost confidence in their own intuition, they increased their dependency on advisers and authority figures. They began relying on their doctors for advice that the doctors were not trained to give.

Christian parents also relied upon their pastors to give them advice on child rearing, but the pastors were not always trained in understanding and communicating God's design for child rearing. "Should I let my baby cry?" "Should I spank or not spank?" Parents were putting their doctors and their pastors on the spot.

Babies of this style of parenting did not "feel right," and they protested this style of management. Behavior problems and discipline problems reached epidemic proportions and were matched by a flurry of remedial books to treat the problems that should not have occurred in the first place. Because mothers and fathers sincerely loved their children, then as now, they read more books about how to raise them. The more they read, the more confused they became. They were constantly faced with the conflict between what they intuitively felt and what they read.

By the early seventies, more and more mothers were realizing that the system which separates mothers and babies simply wasn't working. Something had been taken from mothers, and mothers were determined to get it back. Dramatic and overdue changes in child birthing and child feeding practices occurred.

More and more mothers began bonding with their babies at birth. Most mothers started out breastfeeding their babies and breastfed longer. Parents began giving a more nurturant response to their babies' cries. More and more parents began sleeping with their babies and carrying their babies in a variety of slings and carriers.

Today parents' fear of "spoiling" and of "being manipulated" (especially prevalent among Christian parents) is gradually being replaced by a confident responsiveness that flows from a trust in their basic intuition. And scientific studies are validating what intuitive mothers have known all along: something good happens to parents and babies when they are allowed to get close to each other.

The "super baby" phenomenon, which emphasizes the role of parents as structured educators rather than playful companions and sensitive nurturers, seems to be an overreaction to those lost decades of mother-infant detachment. A bit of balance is needed.

Though our society is now facing new challenges to parenting (economic pressures and marital instability), we are excited about the prospects for parenting over the next two decades. We believe that parents of the nineties want to know their children better and do what is best for parent and child alike. We believe that "what is best" is a style we call *attachment parenting* which Scripture, scientific research, and our own experience all affirm. To encourage parents in understanding and implementing this style of child care is our purpose in writing this book.

CHAPTER ONE

Attachment Parenting

An Overview

"Authors of how-to books are often accused of talking in lofty terms of unrealistic ideals. We know it's risky to talk about ideals. We do not live in an ideal world, and we are all less than ideal people. Yet it's important to know what the ideal is, or how can we come anywhere near reaching it? And much of what we have to share we learned the hard way—from our anything-but-ideal early parenting experience.

BILL: With our first two children I was a lousy dad and an even lousier husband. These two sons came at a time when I was climbing the ladder of professional success. I had bought into the system of medical training that preached profession first and left family a distant second. As a pediatrician, I was dedicated to helping families thrive . . . but my own family barely survived.

I had grown up without a father and somehow had managed to tune out the importance of a father's presence to very young children. I thought my main role was to work hard to support my growing family. After five years of marriage and two children, I had achieved increasing

*professional success, but I was still a failure as a father.
(Martha later told me, "I suspected we were in trouble
when you took a suitcase full of medical books along on
our honeymoon.")*

*When Bobby and Jim were two and four, I was offered
a plum position as chief resident at the Hospital for Sick
Children in Toronto, the largest children's hospital in the
world. I thought I had the world by the tail. I prayed a lot
about my decision, and God responded: "Bill, stop and
take an inventory of where you are."*

*I realized that although I would survive if I rejected
the position, my family wouldn't survive as a unit if I
accepted it. To the surprise of my colleagues and the joy of
my family, I declined the position at the hospital and re-
solved to be content with the private practice of pediatrics
and a part-time teaching position at the hospital. Instead
of a sense of loss, I felt a tremendous sense of gain. What I
had gained was my family. For the first time in my life I
realized that a father cannot make decisions that benefit
him alone.*

*Up until this time I knew only how be a doctor—now I
had to get back into fathering and, for that matter, being a
husband. Our third child, Peter, was born, and I was
around the house more and semi-actively involved—but I
still didn't understand that fathers could have a nurturing role in their children's lives. It took another child,
Heather Hayden Sears, to change my view of parenting
forever. Hayden seemed to come wired with directions
from God reading, "I am giving you this special gift so
that you will finally understand the role of father that I
have created."*

Elements of Attachment Parenting

You'll hear more about Hayden, who was a classic example
of what we term a "high-need baby," in Chapter 5. For
now, we just want to make the point that the Searses are
not living in a world of textbooks and daydreams! Our
notion of "ideal" has grown out of our own real-life experiences, as well as those of our patients.

14

We call the ideal parenting style—that is to say, the approach that works for most families most of the time and is most in accord with God's design as we perceive it in Scripture—"attachment parenting." Attachment parenting helps mother, father, and baby learn to come together as a family—to fit. Fitting together means establishing a relationship that brings out the best in you and your baby.

The elements of attachment parenting are these:

1. A commitment to two relationships—spouse and child.
2. Birth bonding.
3. Openness to the cues of your baby.
4. Prompt response to your baby's cries.
5. Breastfeeding on cue.
6. Weaning in baby's own time.
7. Wearing your baby.
8. Sleep-sharing.
9. Father involvement.

Each of these aspects will be addressed in detail in the chapters to come. We want to stress right at the start that these are simply tools we are offering; you must take them, modify them, and build a style of parenting that is right for you and your children. Not all families are able to make every component a part of their parenting style; for example, a single mother obviously doesn't have the plus of father involvement. Keep in mind that our descriptions are a best-case scenario. If you do not incorporate all nine aspects, it doesn't mean you have failed as a parent—attachment parenting is not an all-or-nothing proposition!

Benefits of Attachment Parenting

The attachment style of parenting is not directed primarily at benefiting the baby or the parent—rather, it aims to benefit the *interaction* between the parent and the infant in the following ways.

1. *Attachment parenting is mutual giving.*

At first you may consider the attachment style of parenting as all giving, giving, giving. To a certain extent, that is true.

Babies are "takers" and parents are "givers"—this is a fact of parenting during the early months. However, the more the parents give to the baby, the more the baby gives back to the parents. Mutual giving leads to a mutual shaping of each other that helps all members of the family fit together.

One example is breastfeeding an infant off to sleep, which we call "nursing down." Mother gives to baby her milk which contains a sleep-inducing substance (only recently identified in the laboratory). Meanwhile the suckling baby stimulates mother to produce more of the hormone *prolactin*, which exerts a tranquilizing effect on the mother. Thus, the mommy puts the baby to sleep and the baby puts the mommy to sleep, an example of how both members of the nursing pair profit when the design is followed.

2. *Attachment parenting helps organize the baby.*
The newborn baby comes disorganized. His sleep-wake patterns are exhaustingly irregular. Most of his cues seem purposeless and hard to decode, and his movements are random and jerky. We have found that attached infants show smoother, more well controlled bodily movements because they are less anxious.

Critics of the attachment style of parenting, those who are afraid of "spoiling" the baby, argue that attachment parenting puts the baby in charge and promotes disorganization. Current research shows that the opposite is true. Infants who spend most of their days in close proximity to their mothers and are allowed to nurse on cue develop more organized sleep-wake cycles. Infant development researchers believe that the mother exerts a regulatory effect on the infant's physiology, and her presence and interaction with the baby are necessary for the optimal functioning of these systems. This style of parenting may, indeed, be where mother is in charge of the infant and discipline begins.

3. *Attachment parenting helps babies (and parents) to thrive.*
All infants grow. Not all infants thrive. Thriving takes growth one step further; it is growth to the fullest potential

of that organism. New research has shown that infants
thrive better with mothers who are sensitively responsive.
Studies in experimental animals show that infants attached
to their mothers show a higher level of growth hormone
and a higher level of the enzymes that promote brain growth.
Separation from the mother or lack of interaction with her
causes the levels of these growth promoting substances to
fall. Studies have shown that infants separated from their
mothers have elevated levels of stress hormone.

We believe the reason attachment parenting helps babies
become more organized and thrive better is that it promotes
the state of *quiet alertness*. This is a behavioral state in
which babies interact with and learn the most from their
environment. It also promotes an attentive stillness in the
infant that allows parents better opportunities to interact
with their baby. Studies have shown a direct relationship
between the percentage of time a newborn is in the quiet
alert state and the degree of mother-infant attachment.

We have noticed that attached infants exhibit more rhythmic, fluid, purposeful movements. The attachment style of
parenting leads to a certain harmony, a fluidity of action
between infant and parents. It helps you "go with the flow"
of your infant's needs and helps your infant "go with the
flow" of your lifestyle. It seems that the mother directs the
energy of the baby toward more purposeful behavior and
thus acts as the baby's conservator of energy. Disorganized
infants spend less time in quiet interaction and therefore
profit less from stimulation from their environment. These
infants also do not bring out the best in their care-giver
parents.

4. *Attachment parenting promotes cognitive development.*
An infant's brain doubles its volume by one year. As the
brain grows, nerve cells called *neurons* proliferate, resem-
bling miles of tangled electrical wires. The disorganized
newborn comes with much of this wiring not yet connected.
During the first year, these neurons grow longer and connect with other neurons to make circuits that enable baby
to think and develop more skills.

Numerous studies by infant development specialists have shown that a secure mother-infant attachment and an appropriately responsive environment enhance brain development. We will discuss how attachment parenting stimulates your baby's mind in Chapter 10.

5. *Attachment parenting promotes mutual shaping.*
Shaping is a psychological term for the process whereby an individual's personality, character, or temperament is molded so that he can best fit into and thrive in his environment. The mutual shaping of behavior by parents and infant is well illustrated in the development of how we learn to communicate with our baby.

Baby's early communication is a language of needs. Crying and smiling are the two main tools used by the infant to communicate needs and reinforce responses to them. Parents gradually learn the language of baby's needs. On the surface they appear to undergo a regression to the level of the baby. They act, talk, and think down to the baby's level, learning the subtle art of non-verbal communication. The family first learns to respond to the language of the baby . . . but eventually the baby learns to speak the language of the family. The baby then learns to act, talk, and think up to the parents' level.

In other words, the parents first become like the baby in order that the baby can more easily become like the parents, and both develop communication skills that neither had before. Infant development researchers consider this phenomenon of mutual shaping one of the most important aspects of developing the fit.

6. *Attachment parenting promotes the spiritual development of the Christian child and the Christian parent.*
During our interviews with parents in preparation for writing this book, we asked parents, "What has this style of parenting done for you?" The most common response was, "We are now more *sensitive*." Parents develop an inner feeling of rightness, some inner balance in which they have a heightened sense of right and wrong. Injustices, wrong-

doings, and wrong decisions bother them more. In essence, they develop a healthy guilt. They develop such a strong internal feeling of rightness that they *feel wrong* when they *act wrong* and *feel right* when they *act right*. Their consciences become more finely tuned.

Attachment parenting also promotes sensitivity in the child. The infant who grows up in a responsive environment with his needs consistently and predictably met develops an internal feeling of rightness which forms the basis of his own Christian conscience later on.

The trust that the infant learns toward his parents lays a foundation for his willingness to trust God. A child must first learn how to trust his earthly parents whom he can see and feel before he can learn to trust his Heavenly Father whom he cannot see and feel. The Bible is about trusting God. It is hard to build this concept of trust in God into a child if he has not first experienced the meaning of the term trust through his relationship with his parents.

7. Attachment parenting teaches intimacy.
A child learns to bond to persons, not things. He becomes a "high-touch person in a high-tech world." The infant who is accustomed to being in arms and at breast will receive security and fulfillment from personal relationships. In our opinion, this infant is more likely to become a child who forms meaningful attachments with peers, and in adulthood will be more likely to develop deep intimacy with a mate. Coupled with proper spiritual training, this carries over into forming an intimate relationship with God.

The child, however, who receives most of his nurturing from things is at risk for developing shallow interpersonal relationships and deriving fulfillment from a materialistic world. This child will find it harder to be fulfilled by God.

8. Attachment parenting makes discipline easier.
Practicing this style of parenting actually makes discipline (that word that Christian parents have been waiting for) easier. Because you know your child better, you are able to read your child's behavior more accurately, respond more

appropriately, and intervene before your child gets into trouble. Because your child feels right, he is more likely to act right.

The child who operates from this inner feeling of rightness is more likely to develop a healthy conscience. He feels right when he does right and feels wrong when he does wrong. This style of parenting makes it easier to create an attitude within your child and an atmosphere within your home that makes punishment seldom necessary. When necessary, it is administered more appropriately. Because of their attachment to one another, parent and child trust each other. Trust is the basis of authority, and a trusted authority figure disciplines more effectively.

Our Journey toward Attachment Parenting

Twenty years ago, when we began our practice, we realized we did not know answers to many of the most common questions new parents had: "Should I let my baby cry?" "How long should I nurse?" "Will I spoil my baby by picking him up all the time?"

These were real questions from real parents, but we did not have the answers. You do not learn answers to these questions in medical school or nurse's training, because the questions are not scientific enough. So we became students all over again. We put aside our personal bias and opened ourselves to learning from experienced parents. We felt like putting a sign outside the office door reading, "Dr. Sears, still in training."

We began to keep careful records of which parents seemed to enjoy their children the most, which children seemed the most well disciplined, which parents seemed to know their children the best, and which children seemed to operate from an internal "feeling of rightness." We then kept records as to what these parents did to make these things happen.

We also gathered material from Scripture, going directly to God's Word to see what directions God has given us for parenting our children. We are not biblical scholars (although Bill spent three years in seminary training), but we have prayed daily that God would give us understanding as we read His Word. We also rely heavily on Bible commentaries and biblical scholars whom we have learned to trust.

It never comes as a surprise to us when scientific research confirms both the excellence of God the Creator's design and the principles taught in His Word. Believing that children are too valuable and parents too vulnerable for our advice to be based primarily upon our own opinions, we investigated the most reputable scientific research concerning parenting.

Finally, we have learned from our own experience as the parents of seven children, each with a unique temperament and unique needs. We have had the chance to experiment with various approaches until we found the one that fit for each child. We have not yet "retired" from parenting but are still very much in the mainstream of everyday parenting problems. Stephen, our seventh child, was born while we were writing this book. Thus we come to you not as experts, but as experienced parents who are still learning and eager to share our long experience, with its successes and failures, with new parents who are eager to learn.

Because there are a wide variety of lifestyles and temperaments in children, we have chosen to give you a book which lays the foundation during the first year, thereafter making it easier for parents to adapt to their child's individual temperament and their lifestyle. If you cannot practice all the steps we have suggested, don't worry. Your bottle-fed baby will be just fine, provided there is an attached mother or father at the other end of that bottle! God has made children and parents very resilient, enabling them to adapt to a wide variety of parenting styles in a wide variety of family situations.

CHAPTER TWO

God's Design for Labor and Birth

We have been blessed with seven beautiful children, and we have experienced seven very different labors and births. They have ranged from the full-on experience of technology including spinal anesthesia and forceps delivery to the other end of the spectrum, that of home birth actually attended by only the baby's father, who happens to be a pediatrician, with the midwife on the way to the birth.

We experienced three hospital births and four home births, and each of these experiences has been part of a continuum of learning and growing. We learned from our first hospital birth what we did not want to happen in the next one. We learned between the second and third what we wanted to experience from childbirth itself, so that our third hospital birth was as close to an ideal hospital birth as was possible.

MARTHA: Our quantum leap into the home birth setting came about as a result of personal circumstances which dictated that home birth would actually be the safest option. We lived an hour's drive from the nearest obstetrical facility, and I had a history, at that point, of very fast labors. My third labor lasted eighty minutes from start to finish. I could choose a pre-term induction with its inherent risks, take a chance of delivering a baby in the back seat of a car on a dark two-lane road en route to the hospital, or opt for a planned, prepared, safe home birth.

Each of our home births was different, but they all had the common denominator of feeling right. When I went into labor I did not have to concern myself with anything other than tuning into my body, mind, and spirit and allowing the process of labor and birth to proceed.

I distinctly remember feeling so at peace with the fact that I didn't have to start running around, grabbing a suitcase here, pushing a child away there, packing them off to someone else's care, while I focused my energies on getting away from my nest to the hospital. Instead, I could slowly and comfortably, and at my own pace, feather my nest and climb into it, and climb out again when I felt that I needed to move around. I was totally in harmony with my own body.

We do not believe that home birth is the correct choice for every pregnant couple. In fact, it may not be the correct choice for many. This decision is one that has to be made by each couple after they have informed themselves of their options and prayed for direction. We strongly feel that a properly planned and fully supported hospital birth, preferably in a birthing room setting, can be just as beautiful and fulfilling and peaceful as our home births were.

If a couple is considering a home birth, one of the first questions that must be answered is "Can we ensure that our home birth will be properly attended?" If the answer to that question is negative, then the energies of the couple would be better spent preparing for a good hospital or birth center experience, rather than an improperly attended home birth.

Recently a study of 12,000 women was conducted. Women who delivered their babies in birth centers—nonhospital facilities organized to provide family-centered maternity care for women—were judged to be at low risk of obstetrical complications (*New England Journal of Medicine*). The women chose birth centers because the centers are less expensive than delivering at the hospital and because the women have more control over their birth experiences. The overall cesarean rate was about half the rate found in reports of hospital births in comparable low-risk women.

We have learned much from our seven different birth experiences, and we feel that we can share certain things that we want every couple to be aware of as they plan this important event in their lives.

MARTHA: My experience with birth actually goes back to my days as a student nurse. Part of my obstetrical training was based on the book Childbirth Without Fear *by Dr. Grantly Dick-Read. I read that book with awe and excitement. Everything he said sounded so right, and I eagerly anticipated my chance to participate in a hospital birth.*

I was soon disappointed and disillusioned at the difference between what I had read and what I saw in practice. I remember feeling vaguely uncomfortable and almost totally useless. I was in the labor room with the mothers and sometimes the fathers as well, yet there was very little I could do to help, other than taking vital signs, filling out charts, and attempting some friendly chatter.

No one seemed to know what to do in terms of really helping the mother. She was left pretty much on her own to deal with the forces of her body, yet she was required to do this in a setting that had her at a great disadvantage. She was laboring in bed in a small labor cubicle, her only activity to watch the minute hand move slowly around the face of the clock, punctuated by a wave of pain every three or four minutes.

I didn't learn anything more about birth until I was pregnant and gave birth to my first baby. I attended a hospital childbirth class and learned next to nothing, except what the hospital wanted me to know about being a good patient. I was totally unprepared for what childbirth would actually be like.

With baby number two, I made it my business to take a real childbirth class. I found a private instructor who gave classes in her home, and I felt I was finally on the right track. I got very excited about the potential for helping women in childbirth. I decided after that birth experience that I wanted to be a childbirth educator someday.

Six years later that was exactly what I was doing—becoming a childbirth educator and going through childbirth classes for expected child number three.

Childbirth Since the 19th Century

MARTHA: At this time I came across the second most important book that I had ever read about childbirth: The Joy of Natural Childbirth *by Helen Wessel. (It has since been republished by Bookmates International, Inc., under its original title,* Natural Childbirth and the Christian Family.*) Little did I realize that eight years later I would meet the author of this wonderful book and she would become our mentor in the area of childbirth. Her book should be required reading for every Christian couple anticipating the birth of a child.*

Helen did ample research into the original languages of Scripture as she searched the Bible to find what God has to say about childbirth. In doing so she realized that the Bible consistently calls childbearing a blessing and not a curse. Helen had also discovered Grantly Dick-Read's book. As she described her experience in an article for *Focus on the Family*, "I read it without stopping, tears of joy and relief streaming down my face. Here at last was a doctor who not only understood how a birthing mother might feel, but who gave glory to God for the miracle of giving birth" (*Focus on the Family*, December, 1986, "The Joy of Childbirth").

In this article Helen goes on to describe the dramatic changes that have occurred over the last several decades in childbirth. "The first uses of chloroform for difficult childbirth began in the nineteenth century and soon led to the routine use of anesthesia for all women in labor. The grave risks for both mother and baby that were associated

26

with heavy anesthetics made it necessary for childbirth to move from the home to the hospital.

Mothers needed to be hospitalized to safeguard them against the risks of anesthesia administered during childbirth. A mother was unable to care for or breastfeed her baby for several hours or even days, while recovering from the effects of anesthesia. This led to the establishment of separate nurseries and to the bottle-feeding of all newborns." Helen herself became a victim of this style of childbirth with the birth of her first child, whom she did not even see until the day following the baby's birth.

"Into this milieu," continues Helen, "in 1944, the writing of the English physician, Dr. Grantly Dick-Read, came like a thunderbolt. Though new in the United States, his philosophy was already known and accepted in many parts of the world. He taught that while childbirth is an intensely physical, extremely personal experience, suffering is not an essential part. When a woman learns what sensations to expect, she can relax and flow with them during labor and birth. Alert and responsive to her instincts, she can birth her baby in dignity and peace."

The most important concern of every pregnant women is that she and her baby will be healthy. The next concern is easing the pain of labor. Some people have interpreted Genesis 3:16 to mean that excessive pain in childbirth is not only inevitable but is part of God's plan: "To the woman [God] said, 'I will greatly increase your pains in childbearing; with pain you will give birth to children.'"

According to Helen Wessel, the reference to pain is a misinterpretation. She has found that the same word that is translated *pain* for Eve in childbirth is translated for Adam as *labor* or *toil*. What God is saying in Genesis 3:16 is that women will have to labor or work in childbirth, not that they must suffer pain.

Childbirth Education

In this era of childbirth education, a Christian couple must be very discerning. I Timothy 4:7 says, "Have nothing to do with godless myths and old wives' tales; rather, train yourselves to be godly." Proverbs 23:12 says, "Apply your heart to instruction and your ears to words of knowledge." We use these verses to underline the importance of finding good childbirth education and, we would like to add, good Christian childbirth education.

To quote again from Helen Wessel: "The Lamaze method (expounded in France in 1953) did not become known in the United States until the early 1960s. It differed from Dick-Read's philosophy, not only by substituting scientism for faith, but in another serious way which he did not realize, by introducing self-hypnotism. This hypnotic state is induced by concentrating on specific artificial breathing patterns to be used for long periods of time during the labor, while focusing one's eyes on an object, thus supposedly being distracted from pain. Many Christians believe hypnotism is forbidden in Scripture. Those who either teach Lamaze or take Lamaze childbirth classes need to be aware of its atheistic origins, and also to make sure that hypnotic breathing and focusing of the eyes is not a part of what is taught."

Unfortunately, beginning in the 70s, subtle occult and New Age ideas and practices from the counter-culture began to infiltrate the natural and home birth movements. One of the main influences has been a widely read book, *Spiritual Midwifery*, written in the 1970s by a midwife from the cult group known as "The Farm." This "spirituality" is definitely not of God. Other occult practices include promoting transcendental meditation, chanting of mantras to aid relaxation, and the use of yoga in pregnancy and childbirth.

As Helen became aware of the extent of such occult influences in childbirth circles, she felt led to found Appletree Family Ministries, which provides materials for childbirth education. The organization receives its name from the title of her second book, *Under the Apple Tree: Marriage, Birthing, and Parenting*.

There is also a guide for group study of this most sacred event. What better way to prepare for a baby's arrival than by praying and studying the Scriptures with other Christians? Clearly God intends for us to be focused on Him throughout the whole process of pregnancy, labor, and birth.

> "Yet you brought me out of the womb, you made me trust in you even at my mother's breast, from birth I was cast upon you, from my mother's womb you have been my God." (Psalm 22: 9, 10)

> "From birth I have relied on you, you brought me forth from my mother's womb, I will ever praise you." (Psalm 71:6)

In choosing a birthing environment and childbirth education classes, here are some guidelines to help decide if you are choosing correctly. These recommendations are taken from a report on "Appropriate Technology for Birth," published by the World Health Organization in April, 1985.

- There is no evidence that a cesarean section is necessary after a previous transverse low segment cesarean section birth. Vaginal deliveries after a cesarean should normally be encouraged wherever emergency surgical capacity is available.
- There is no evidence that routine electronic fetal monitoring during labor has a positive effect on the outcome of pregnancy.
- There is no indication for pubic shaving or a pre-delivery enema.
- Pregnant women should not be put in a lithotomy position (flat on the back) during labor or delivery. They should be encouraged to walk during labor and each women must freely decide which position to adopt during delivery.
- The systematic use of episiotomy (incision to enlarge the vaginal opening) is not justified.
- Birth should not be induced (started artificially) for convenience, and the induction of labor should be reserved for specific medical indications. No geographic region should have rates of induced labor over ten percent.

I During delivery, the routine administration of analgesic or anesthetic drugs that are not specifically required to correct or prevent a complication in delivery should be avoided.

I Artificial early rupture of the membranes as a routine process is not scientifically justified.

I The healthy newborn must remain with the mother whenever both their conditions permit it. No process of observation of the healthy newborn justifies a separation from the mother.

I The immediate beginning of breastfeeding should be promoted, even before the mother leaves the delivery room.

Labor Support

To help you implement these guidelines, I would like to offer several suggestions. First, consider finding the services of a labor support person who can be with you throughout your labor and birth, especially if you are having a hospital birth. She should be a woman well experienced in laboring and birthing, one who has had childbirth experiences of her own and who has educated herself in the art and the science of assisting women in birth. She could be a midwife or a childbirth educator.

Studies show that couples attended by a labor support person have fewer complications, need less pitocin augmentation, have significantly shorter labors, have less incidence of cesarean section, and have fewer infants requiring special care after birth.

Your labor support person will not take the place of the father of the baby. Rather, her presence will free the father from the pressure of having to recall everything that he learned in the childbirth class. He can spend his energy supporting his wife emotionally and physically, as he feels able. For fathers who feel uncertain of their role, the labor support person can provide guidance and reassurance.

She should be familiar with various labor methods and willing to attend one or two of your childbirth classes. She should be familiar with labor coping techniques and comfort measures for pregnancy, labor, and postpartum. She should understand the various obstetrical procedures and be familiar with possible complications, and techniques for handling them, especially as they would relate to cesarean section prevention. She should be able to advise you on newborn procedures and how to avoid unnecessary mother-baby separation, as well as how to establish early breastfeeding.

It is ideal if a Christian couple can locate Christian childbirth classes and a Christian labor support person, one who will be able to support the couple spiritually as well.

An Approach to Pain in Childbirth

Since pain in childbirth is the major concern of most couples, it is important to understand the fear-tension-pain syndrome described by Dr. Dick-Read. Pain is not an intrinsic part of every labor; *sensation* is. Discomfort, minor to acute, may be part of most every labor and birth. Acute discomfort is painful and leads to real suffering if not handled properly.

The pain of labor is pain with a purpose. If the pain is causing a woman to *suffer,* then she won't relax, and her tension and fear will actually interfere with labor, possibly resulting in "failure to progress," which leads to cesarean section. But if pain is perceived as positive and is managed correctly, there can be minimal tension and fear, and labor will progress normally as God intended it to.

Our goal is not to obliterate totally the sensations of childbirth, because a certain amount of hurting is natural. There are moments in any childbirth that will be perceived as, "It hurts." But God never intended woman to *suffer* in childbirth; rather, He intended her to work hard. As we all know, any hard work can at times be perceived as painful!

The big enemy here is fear. When we are not able to trust God during a time of trial, fear becomes our enemy. We encourage couples to search the Scriptures and write down verses with special meaning on index cards. The cards can be used during labor as a means of prayer, helping the couple through the rough times that will come in any labor.

31

The following verses are some we have found helpful:

"So do not fear, for I am with you; do not be dismayed, for I am your God. I will strengthen you and help you; I will uphold you with my righteous right hand." (Isaiah 41:10)

"Delight yourself in the Lord and he will give you the desires of your heart. Commit your way to the Lord; trust in him and he will do this." (Psalm 37:4, 5)

"Cast all your anxiety on him because he cares for you." (I Peter 5:7)

"There is no fear in love. But perfect love drives out fear, because fear has to do with punishment. The man who fears is not made perfect in love." (I John 4:18)

"Peace I leave with you; my peace I give you. I do not give to you as the world gives. Do not let your hearts be troubled and do not be afraid." (John 14:27)

Pain as Partner

Our American culture has taught us to fear pain and immediately look for relief from it. We have not learned to understand the pain of labor, to relax into it and work with it.

One of the biggest lessons I learned from my childbirth experiences was to see what happened when my body resisted a contraction when it hurt. When I braced *against* a contraction, it immediately became much more painful. As I recognized this process occurring, I made a definite effort to do just the opposite; I released my muscles rather than bracing them. I let them go. I allowed my body to go with the contraction. The painful negative sensations vanished, and all that was left was the feeling of work, the feeling of *pressure*.

How interesting that Scripture says the same thing that I discovered: "A woman giving birth to a child has pain because her time has come; but when her baby is born she forgets the anguish because of her joy that a child is born into the world." (John 16:21)

I could accept the word pain, because I have learned about the sensations of childbirth. But the term anguish always bothered me because this, in my mind, translated into suffering. Then I learned that the Greek work for anguish, *thlipsis*, can also be translated "pressure." Of course! I could understand that. There is definitely the sensation of pressure in childbirth. And the Scripture is indeed right; those feelings, those memories of pressure are immediately wiped out upon being presented with your newborn.

The sensations that a woman in labor experiences should be a friend, an ally, telling her that her body is working strongly and that her baby will soon be born. Labor is a strange combination of both pleasure and pain, with a very fine line dividing the two. Too many women concentrate so much on the painful aspect of labor that they miss the pleasure part. Research shows that women who consciously experience pain (not suffering) describe more emotionally positive experiences than women who are anesthetized.

Eliminating all labor sensations, all bodily sensations, even if they can be perceived as painful, may actually inhibit the process of labor. There is a system of regulation of labor involving the body's production of hormones, which are responsible for the activity of labor. Pain can actually give important messages to the woman to assist her in working with her body.

It can tell her, for instance, when it is time to change positions or time to start moving around. The feedback that a woman gets from her body through these "painful" sensations can be very desirable and valuable, maybe even reassuring. For example, she can realize that with stronger contractions and "more pain" she is closer to the birth and closer to seeing her baby. By perceiving pain as an ally rather than an enemy to be resisted, it becomes tolerable.

In order to accept some hurting as a natural part of childbirth, something that should be worked with and not resisted, women need to have permission to express their physical sensations. They need to feel free to groan and moan and even cry out without causing panic in those around them. It can actually be relaxing for a woman to express verbally what her body is experiencing internally, if she knows her attendants will understand and encourage her.

MARTHA: I remember the low groaning sounds that came from my mouth, actually from somewhere deep inside of me, during the births of my babies. At the time, I worried that these noises would bother the people around me, that it would make them think that I was in terrible trouble or that I needed them to do something. I knew that I didn't need anything except to continue going in the direction that my body was moving. Part of that direction was to be able to vocalize what I was feeling.

The people working with the woman in labor need to be comfortable with the idea of pain so that they can allow her to experience it and not feel that they have to rescue her from it. She needs to see herself as strong and able to work through her labor. She does not need to see herself as a victim of pain. And of course, at whatever point in time the perception of pain does change to "suffering," then it is time to reevaluate the progress of the labor and make some intelligent and wise decisions about what to do next.

Position During Delivery

The only reason that modern women think that childbirth should be performed on their backs is because this is the only position that a totally anesthetized woman is capable of, and so this is how the hospitals had to do it. This should never happen in a natural childbirth.

In a study of childbirth in ancient and indigenous art by Janet Issacs Ashford (*Childbirth Alternatives Quarterly*, Winter 1988, Vol. IX, No. 2), the writer identifies the "classic birthing pose" that we see throughout history. The classic pose consists of a mother in an upright posture with a helper behind her supporting her bodily and a midwife in front with arms outstretched to receive the baby. These three figures arranged in this close supportive pose are seen again and again across time and culture. It was not until childbirth went into the hospital and became anesthetized that we took for granted that a woman should give birth flat on her back.

Getting in Shape for Childbirth

Remember, labor is a physical event, and if you have not prepared yourself for it through physical conditioning and prenatal exercises, you may have to suffer the consequences. The best physical preparation, in addition to faithfully doing the prenatal exercises recommended in your childbirth class, is to walk briskly for at least one or two miles a day.

If you can do this faithfully from the moment you learn you are pregnant, your body will have the proper fitness it needs when it is time to perform the most intense work you will ever be asked to do. Although the writers of the following verses didn't have childbirth in mind, the words seem apropos.

> "She girds herself with strength and makes her arms strong." (Proverbs 31:17)

> "Be ye strong therefore, and let not your hands be weak: For your work shall be rewarded." (II Chronicles 15:7)

Medical Intervention in Childbirth

Pain medication and medical intervention are, of course, tools that are available if they are ultimately needed. If they need to be called upon, there should be no shame connected with that. For example, if a woman does require anesthesia or cesarean section because of failure to progress, she often experiences feeling of failure and utter disgrace. It is true that these things sometimes happen unnecessarily, but there are situations where cesarean section is a relief from suffering or even a lifesaving procedure. The trust that you have in your body and the trust that you have in

God will stand you in good stead in being able to accept these types of procedures if they do become truly necessary.

Usually extreme medical intervention does not become necessary until other techniques have been put into effect. These may include movements and repositioning of the mother, counter pressure from the father or labor support person onto the labor woman's back, the use of superficial heat and cold, touch massage and relaxation. The ultimate in childbirthing comfort, soaking in a full tub of warm water, can greatly decrease the perception of pain from the contractions of labor. Emotional support, spiritual support from prayer, relaxation skills, deep relaxed breathing, and the use of music can greatly decrease the need for much more risky pain medications. Those techniques may not take away the sensations entirely, but remember that that is not the goal. They can keep a woman from suffering, and make the difference between achieving a natural vaginal birth versus needing a cesarean birth due to failure to progress.

MARTHA: With the birth of our last baby, I personally experienced the benefits of water labor. I typically have fast (one to two hours) labors that only become intense in the short time before pushing, and then after two or three pushes the baby is born. Two of my labors have been "longer" (four to five hours), but of such low intensity that I was actually lulled into thinking it really wasn't labor until I was very close to pushing.

However, with baby number seven, this pattern changed. After four hours of mild, easy labor, I began experiencing an intense hurt low in the front. This was a signal to my body that something needed attention. If it had been pain in my back, the all-fours position would have helped. I tried that position anyway, but it only hurt more.

Then my midwife suggested I get into the water. As I slipped into the warm water, I felt my limbs relax. I experimented with different positions and finally found one that allowed me to just let go and float from my shoulders down so my whole torso and pelvis relaxed as well. At that point, total relaxation, the pain literally melted away—better than Demerol! The buoyancy did for me what I was not able to achieve by myself.

The experience of total release accompanied by total relief was amazing. I stayed in the water for about an hour until I recognized signals of the pushing stage. At that point I decided to get out of the water. I lay down on the bed on my left side and gave birth after two pushes.

As the baby emerged we discovered the reason for the pain. The baby's hand was presenting alongside his head—two parts coming through at once. My body needed total relaxation to allow my muscles to give way to a larger than usual presenting part. The birth itself went smoothly and we rejoiced once again in the miracle of God's creation.

CHAPTER THREE

Getting to Know Your Newborn

Every new mother wonders, "How will I ever take care of this little human being? Will I be a good mother?" The intense desire to be the mother that God intended you to be, coupled with your intense love for your newborn, are likely to bring out normal feelings of doubt. Keep in mind that God wouldn't have created a system of mother-newborn care that doesn't work. We believe that God put within the mother all the necessary capabilities to nurture her child. And God put within the tiny newborn a signaling system that will alleviate your very present fear, "How will I know what she needs?"

This system will work, but only if we provide the conditions by which it was designed to operate. In this chapter we will present those conditions which allow the God-given system of mother-infant care to get the right start.

Getting the Right Start
Step 1. Bond with your baby immediately after birth.
The way in which mother and baby get started sets the tone of how quickly they get to know each other. Immediately

after delivery, unless prevented by a medical complication, request that your newborn be placed skin to skin on your abdomen, baby's head nestling on your breast, and baby's back and head covered by a warm towel. (This is not just good psychology; it is good medicine. Newborns easily get cold. Draping baby over mother, tummy to tummy, cheek to breast, allows a natural heat transfer from mother to infant.)

The first hour after birth is a prime time of receptivity for mother and infant, a sensitive period in which mother and newborn are programmed to get to know each other. Within minutes after birth, the newborn enters a state of *quiet alertness*—the state in which, researchers have discovered, a baby is most able to take from and give to her environment. During this alert stage, the baby looks directly at the mother's eyes and snuggles at the mother's breasts.

Don't be surprised if, during this first meeting, your newborn seems to be relatively still. It's almost as if she is so enthralled by what she sees, hears, and feels that she doesn't want to waste any energy squirming! During this early bonding, your baby drinks in the sound of your voice, the feel of your warm skin, and the taste of your breast. Within minutes after birth the infant begins to feel to whom she belongs. Within an hour or two after birth, the baby contentedly drifts into a deep sleep.

Think about the very important fact your baby has learned during this first meeting: Distress is followed by comfort. She is learning the single most valuable lesson in infant development—that she can trust her environment.

Here are some suggestions to help you and your baby better enjoy this initial bonding experience.

After the delivery room personnel have attended to mother and baby (and assuming both mother and baby are well), *request some private time alone*—just the three of you. This is a special time of family intimacy which should not be interrupted by trivial hospital routines or diluted by depressing medications.

Breastfeed your baby right after delivery. The baby's sucking and licking the nipple releases the hormone *oxytocin* into the mother's bloodstream. Oxytocin causes the uterus to contract and lessens the complication of postpartum bleeding. Some babies have a strong desire to suck the breast immediately after birth; others are content simply to lick the nipple.

Touch your baby. Gently stroke your baby, touch her whole body. We have observed how mothers and fathers touch their newborn differently. A mother may stroke her baby's entire body with a gentle caress of her fingertips, while a father often places his entire hand on his baby's head as if symbolizing his commitment to protect the life he has fathered.

Beside being fun, stroking has medical benefits. The skin is the largest organ of the human body, and very rich in nerve endings. At a crucial transition time in baby's entry into the world, when breathing patterns are often very irregular, stroking stimulates the newly born baby to breath more rhythmically. Your touch has therapeutic value.

Gaze at your baby. Your newborn can see best within the distance of twelve inches, which, incidentally, is the usual distance from mother's nipple to her eyes during breast-feeding. When you look at your baby, place her in the enface position, meaning that your eyes and your baby's eyes meet in the same vertical plane.

During the first hour after birth, babies' eyes are wide open, as if wanting to relate to their newly found world. Ask the nurses to delay putting ointment in your baby's eyes until after the bonding period, since this may blur baby's vision at the very time she is developing her first impression of you. Staring into your baby's eyes may make you feel you don't want to release this little person that you have labored so hard to bring into the world. And guess what . . . you don't have to!

What if you can't be with your baby immediately following her birth? What about the newborn who for some reason, such as arriving prematurely or by cesarean delivery, is temporarily separated from her mother? Is the baby permanently affected by the loss of early contact, or can one make up for what the baby has missed?

The first few moments of attachment are not like instant glue, cementing a mother-baby relationship on the spot. There are many steps that must be taken before a strong attachment develops. Immediate close contact during this biologically sensitive period simply gives this attachment a head start.

We believe that God has built into His design a great deal of resiliency and adaptability. We suspect that as soon as mothers and babies are reunited, a strong mother-infant attachment can compensate for the loss of this early opportunity for bonding.

Step 2. Room in with your baby.
Bonding begins in the delivery room; it does not end there. Unless prevented by a medical complication, healthy mothers and healthy babies should be together from the time of birth to the time of discharge from the hospital. Rooming in with your baby allows mother and baby to begin developing the communication network that God has designed. Here's how it works.

All babies are born with special traits called *attachment-promoting features and behaviors*, designed to alert the care giver to the baby's presence and draw the care giver, magnet-like, toward the baby. These include the roundness of baby's eyes, cheeks, and body, the softness of baby's skin, the relative bigness of baby's eyes and, most important of all, baby's early language—her cries.

Rooming in with your baby allows these attachment-promoting qualities to work. Let's examine the most intense of these attachment-promoting behaviors, the baby's cries.

A baby's cry is designed for the survival of the baby and the developing of the mother instinct. The opening sounds of the baby's cries activate a mother's emotions. This is physical as well as psychological.

Upon hearing her baby cry, a mother's blood flow to her breasts increases, and she feels the urge to pick up and nurse her baby. This is one of the strongest examples of how a biological signal of the baby triggers a biological response in the mother. There is no other signal in the world which triggers such intense emotions in a mother as her baby's cry. At no other time in a child's life will the language of the child so forcefully stimulate the mother to act.

Picture what happens when a baby and her mother room together. Baby begins to cry. Mother, because she is there and attuned to baby, immediately picks up and nurses her infant. Baby stops crying. The next time baby awakens, squirms, grimaces, and cries, mother responds in the same manner. The next time mother notices her baby's pre-crying cues. When baby awakens, squirms, and grimaces, mother picks up and nurses baby *before* she has to cry. Mother has learned to read her baby's signals and respond appropriately.

After rehearsing this dialogue many times during the rooming-in period, mother and baby work as a team. Baby learns to cue better, mother learns to respond better. After a couple days of this stimulus-response activity, mother may begin to notice amazing biological changes triggered by her baby's cry.

In response to baby's cry and the appearance and feel of her baby, her breasts begin to feel full and she feels the sensation of milk being released from the back part of her breasts to the front. Mother and her rooming-in infant are beginning to be in biological harmony. How magnificently God has designed this start-up system to work, as long as we create the conditions which allow it to get into motion!

Contrast this rooming-in scene with that of the infant cared for in the hospital nursery. Picture the newborn infant lying in a plastic box. She awakens, hungry, and cries along with twenty other hungry babies in plastic boxes, who have by now all managed to awaken each other. A kind and caring nurse, but an individual who has no biological attachment to the baby, hears the cries and responds as soon as time permits. The crying, hungry baby is taken to her mother in due time. The problem is that a baby's cry has two phases: the early sounds, which have an attachment-promoting quality, and the later sounds of an unattended cry, which are more disturbing to listen to and may actually promote avoidance.

The mother, who has missed the opening scene because she was not present when her baby started to cry, is nonetheless expected to give a nurturing response to her baby some minutes later. By this time the infant has either given up crying and gone to sleep or is now greeting mother with even more intense and upsetting wails. The mother hears only the cries that are more likely to illicit agitated concern rather than tenderness. Though she has a comforting breast to offer the baby, she may be so tied up in knots that her milk won't release, and the baby cries even harder.

As she grows to doubt her ability to comfort her baby, the infant may wind up spending even more time in the nursery. This separation leads to more missed cues and more breaks in the attachment between mother and baby. They leave the hospital together, more or less strangers.

We have observed the following medical benefits in babies who stay attached to their mother for the first few days after birth: these babies developed less jaundice and lost less weight; their mothers' milk came in twenty-four to forty-eight hours sooner; the infant distress syndrome (fussiness, colic, incessant crying) was less common than with infants cared for in central nurseries; and mothers developed more confidence and mature coping skills with their babies' crying. Nursery-reared babies learned to cry harder; rooming-in babies learned to cry *better.*

Step 3. Nest in with your baby.
The next two weeks, which we call the nesting-in period, is a time for mother and baby to refine their mutual attachment qualities. Here are some tips to help you and your baby get the most out of the fitting-in period.

Define priorities. We advise mothers in childbirth classes, "Don't take your nightgown off for two weeks. Sit in your rocking chair and let yourself be mothered!" Here are our recommendations.

TEN COMMANDMENTS FOR THE POSTPARTUM MOTHER

1. Thou shalt not give up thy baby to strange care givers.
2. Thou shalt not cook, clean house, do laundry, or entertain.
3. Thou shalt be given adulation.
4. Thou shalt remain clothed in thy nightgown and sit in thy rocking chair.
5. Thou shalt honor thy husband with his share of household chores.
6. Thou shalt take long walks in green pastures, eat good food, and drink much water.
7. Thou shalt not have before you strange and unhelpful visitors.
8. Thou shalt groom thy hair and adorn thy body with attractive robes.
9. Thou shalt be allowed to sleep when baby sleeps.
10. Thou shalt not have prophets of bad baby advice before you.

Most parents are not adequately prepared for how much care a newborn baby requires. The first couple weeks are usually described as "wonderful but exhausting."

Moms, at no other time in your life will you experience so many changes so fast. Your body is undergoing tremendous changes, both adjusting from having just given birth and preparing to continue nourishing your baby. You will experience tremendous changes in your sleep schedule, eating patterns, and type of work. This is why it is extremely important, for both you and baby, temporarily to shelve and eliminate interference which may siphon off the energy needed for the two of you.

Find dad's role in the nesting period. Dad, when mother and baby come home from the hospital or birthing place, make your "nest" as conducive to mothering as possible. Take over the housekeeping, or hire some help if you can afford it. Because of the tremendous physiological and emotional changes going on in the postpartum mother, you will find her emotions very unstable. An organized environment helps foster an organized emotional state in mother and baby.

It is a good idea to stroll around the house each day and take inventory of actual and potential problems that may upset the mother—and then take care of these problems! Remember that upsets felt by the mother may be transferred to the baby.

Give specific instructions to older siblings to pick up after themselves. Tell them why particular attention to tidiness is so helpful at this time. After all, they are future mothers and fathers; they should learn that the postpartum period is a time when the whole family gives to mom. It is a time for all those little and big takers to become givers.

Ward off "prophets of bad baby advice." This is your baby, not someone else's. Love for her baby makes a new mother particularly vulnerable to advice that implies that she might not be doing the best thing for her baby. Conflicting advice is confusing even to the most confident mother. This is dad's opportunity to shine. If you sense that outside advice is upsetting your wife, protect her against it and support her style of mothering.

Be open to the cues of your baby and respond according to your intuitive feelings. Remember, every baby comes wired with attachment-promoting behaviors which enable her to communicate her level of need to her care givers. Parents also come wired with a certain intuitive level of giving and responding. Part of developing the fit during these early weeks is to match the need level of the baby and the response level of the parents.

Baby gives a cue, and the mother and father, because they are open and tuned in to the baby, respond to the cue. In time you and your baby begin to flow together, developing a harmony between cue and response. As all members of the family repeatedly rehearse this communication, the baby learns to cue better, the parents learn to respond better, and the communication network is in harmony. The family is learning to fit.

CHAPTER FOUR

Understanding Your Baby's Cries

Nearly every day we get a phone call from a new mother asking, "Am I spoiling my baby by picking him up when he cries? My friends tell me to let him cry it out, but I can't."

In preparation for our book *The Fussy Baby*, I sent out several hundred questionnaires asking parents about advice they received concerning their parenting styles. One of the questions was, "What advice do you get about responding to your baby's cries?" The most common responses were:

"Crying is good for his lungs."

"Let him cry it out; he's manipulating you."

"He's got to learn to be independent."

We also asked how this advice made them feel. Their most frequent responses were:

"It goes against my instincts."

"I can't do it."

"It doesn't feel right to me."

"I can't let him cry when I know I have the means to comfort him."

Ninety-five percent of the mothers said that the advice to let their babies cry did not feel right to them! After twenty years in pediatric practice and surviving the cries of our seven infants, we have learned to place great value on what mothers call "gut feelings." Therefore we concluded that ninety-five percent of mothers couldn't be wrong!

Our questionnaire also showed us that there is a disturbing conflict between what mothers feel and what other people are telling them to do. Because a new mother wishes to do the best for her baby, she is vulnerable to this advice and therefore is left confused.

To clear up the confusion between what mothers feel and what they hear, we spent some time studying the medical literature on the signal value of the infant's cry. We also studied our own patients to understand why some infants cry better and some parents respond more sensitively.

The Biology of Crying

The infant's cry is designed for the survival of the baby and the development of the parents. It is a two-way communication network in which the infant is programmed to give a signal, and parents—the receivers—are programmed to respond. Let's examine both parts of this uniquely designed communication network.

In the first few months of life, a baby's needs are greatest at a time when his skills to communicate these needs are least. A baby cannot tell us what he needs. To fill the gap in time until the baby is able to "speak our language," he has been given a language called a cry, and this is how it works. The baby senses a need. The realization of this need reflexively triggers the sudden inspiration of air, followed by a forceful expiration. The expelled air passes the vocal cords, and the vibrating cords produce a sound we call a cry.

A cry is not just a sound; it is a signal. Cries are triggered by needs, and babies will use different signals for different needs. The stronger the need-stimulus, the more forcefully the baby expels air, and the vocal cords vibrate more rapidly. This accounts for the difference in the quality of the sounds produced. Researchers call these unique sounds *cry prints*, which are as unique to each baby as fingerprints.

Voice researchers have concluded that the infant cry meets the four qualities of a perfect signal. First, the cries of early infancy are of reflex origin; they are *automatic*. They flow naturally in response to a need. The tiny infant does not have to stop and think, "Now, what kind of cry will get me fed?" As these initial reflex cries are responded to, they are later refined into more purposeful and deliberate crying, and then, as the infant learns to trust his communicating ability (and your responding ability), the crying is even better refined into true language. In essence, the baby learns to "cry better."

Second, the signal is *easily generated;* the baby initiates crying with very little effort. Third, this signal is *disturbing* enough to alert the care giver to attend to the baby, but not so disturbing as to promote an avoidance response. Fourth, the cry *vanishes* when the need for it has passed. These features make the infant cry a perfect signal designed by God to insure the survival of His young.

What is even more fascinating than God's design of the infant cry as the perfect signal is His design of the effect the cry has on the parents, especially the mother. It seems that God put within mothers a biological receiver that is triggered by her baby's cries, as if He were ensuring some biological guarantee that His young would be taken care of. By responding to your baby's cries from your heart and following your God-given biological intuition, you develop one of the most important parenting qualities—*sensitivity*.

What happens if a mother follows the restraining advice to let her baby "cry it out"? In essence, both mother and baby lose. The opening sounds of a baby's cry are an attachment-promoting behavior designed to release a biological attachment behavior from the mother. If the mother gives an immediate nurturant response to her baby's cries, the baby's cries stop or at least lessen. Mother feels right because she has followed her biological intuition and in so doing increased her sensitivity.

Turning to the other side of the mother-baby crying equation, the baby, because his cries were immediately

51

listened to, learned to stop crying. The sensitivity level of the mother and the trust level of the baby became better developed.

If, however, the mother restrains herself from following her intuition, both members of this communication network lose. By going against her own biological intuition, the mother becomes less sensitive to her baby's cries (and eventually to her baby). And contrary to popular belief that unanswered cries will stop, research has show that "unanswered" babies cry harder. The longer the response time of the mother, the more disturbing the nature of the baby's cry becomes. Eventually the pair becomes what we call "over the hill." Baby's cry takes on such a disturbing quality that, instead of having the attachment-promoting qualities of the early and trusting type of cry, it takes on a disturbing quality and promotes an avoidance response from the listener.

As a result, baby learns to cry harder, mother learns to respond less sensitively, and the pair drifts apart. Baby loses trust in his natural communication mechanism and either shuts it down and does not optimally cry, or takes on alternative survival mechanisms which are less natural signals, thereby invoking less natural responses.

The mother also loses trust in her ability to read her baby's signals and develops a case of what we in the child care trade refer to as the "Doctor-tell-me-what-to-do's." The sad fact is, the doctor doesn't know. He or she is outside this communication system, having no biological attachment to the baby.

Teaching Your Baby to Cry Better

The following suggestions are aimed at helping your baby develop means of communication other than crying and to develop your sensitivity to reading your baby, creating a communication system in which your baby does not *have* to cry.

1. *Develop a healthy attitude toward your baby's cries.* Think of them as a signal to be valued, not a habit to be broken.

This starts your crying communication network off on the right note. Your baby's cries are a signal to be responded to, mellowed out, and then fine-tuned into better communication skills.

2. *Act, don't think.* When you first hear your baby cry, react spontaneously according to the first feeling that your intuition prompts. Don't stop and think, "Why is he crying? Is he trying to manipulate me? Will I spoil him?" This type of cry analysis comes much later, after your communication network is well established.

It isn't as important to know why your baby is crying as it is simply to respond to your baby. Giving an immediate nurturant response to your baby's cry helps to develop your intuition, so that eventually you will better understand why your baby is crying and better trust your intuitive response. In time you will develop a wisdom about crying, knowing when to respond immediately and when you can comfortably delay your response.

Newborns who receive an immediate nurturing response to their cries eventually cry less frequently and with less intensity. Even when they do cry, their cries are less disturbing.

3. *Examine your after-cry feeling.* A new mother who had followed the restraint advice of a well-meaning friend shared her feelings with us. "One night when he woke up with his usual demanding cry at 3:00 a.m., I decided to let him cry it out. Boy, was he mad! I'll never do that again. I felt so guilty. His crying was bad for both of us."

We feel that God, because He cares about mothers, babies, and fathers, has provided parents with some internal sensor that feels right when you respond right and feels wrong when you respond wrongly. This feeling is a healthy guilt which tells you that you have violated your internal sensor and have been left with the resulting feeling of "unrightness."

Whenever a mother tells us, "My baby's cry doesn't bother me anymore," we red-tag that baby's chart, because somewhere down the road mother and baby may be in trouble.

4. *Anticipate baby's needs before crying begins.* An experienced mother who practices attachment parenting told us, "My baby seldom cries. He doesn't need to." The ultimate in cry-mellowing is to be so tuned in to your baby's cues that he doesn't have to cry to get what he needs.

5. *Beware of those who advise you to let your baby cry it out.* It is easy for someone who has no biological attachment to the baby to preach this wrongful advice. That old line "Crying is good for his lungs" is supported neither by common sense nor scientific research. Studies show absolutely no beneficial effect of crying. Actually, crying causes a worrisome increase in baby's heart rate. The oxygen level in baby's blood may be diminished; some may even pass out from prolonged crying. A father who is a professional researcher summed up this bit of advice by saying, "Crying is as good for the lungs as bleeding is for the veins."

Another bit of misguided "wisdom" is this: "If you pick him up every time he cries, he'll become a whiny child and never stop crying." This is a carryover from an old school of behavioral psychology which based its erroneous preaching more on personal opinion than on scientific research. Studies have shown that when babies' cries are promptly attended to early on, these babies actually learn to cry and whine less as older infants and toddlers. Some researchers have shown that too much unattended-to crying delays the development of visual-motor skills in the baby, perhaps by causing the baby to divert so much energy into learning his own self-soothing skills.

The biblical, scientific, and time-tested practice of giving nurturant response to your baby's cry is a God-given design for the survival of the baby and the development of the parent which lays the foundation for the development of even better communication skills. Baby and parents learn to trust one another.

All through Scripture, we see in the relationship between people and God examples of one in need crying out to One in a position to fill that need. Implied is a *trust*, an anticipation that God will hear the cries and respond sensitively.

Scripture never says, " and God let them cry it out!" Rather, we read words like these of the psalmist: "To the Lord I cry aloud, and He answers me" (Psalm 3:4). Let us model our response as parents on that of our perfect, loving heavenly Father.

CHAPTER FIVE

Understanding Your Baby's Temperament

"I wonder what our baby is going to be like," most parents-
to-be muse while they're waiting out those nine long months.
It won't be long before you will have a clue about the temperament of your baby. (We use the term "temperament"
to mean how your baby behaves, how she acts, the intent
within her that makes her act the way she does.)

Your baby will probably receive certain temperament
labels such as easy, difficult, mellow, fussy, or demanding.
With time the child's reactions to the environment and the
environment's influence upon the child develops this inner
temperament into personality—the outward expression of
the child's inner temperament.

Perhaps the baby that you had hoped for is not the baby
you got! In this chapter we will discuss why your baby
acts the way she does and offer you practical suggestions
on coping with the less than perfect baby.

Nature vs. Nurture
For decades, psychologists have debated the nature versus
nurture question: Is it primarily heredity or environment

that determines the child's temperament? Today most scientists agree that a child's temperament is not a blank slate onto which care givers can write a set of rules that will cause a child to act any way the care givers wish. Neither is the child's temperament permanently cast in cement. Temperament is due to *both* nature (genetic influences) and nurture (the parenting style of the care-giving environment).

The Bible alludes to the individuality of a child's temperament. "For you created my inmost being; you knit me together in my mother's womb" (Psalm 139:13). "Train a child in the way he should go. . ." (Proverbs 22:6). An infant comes wired with a temperament that is to a large extent genetically determined and, to an extent that we will never completely understand, God has had His handiwork in the formation of every child's temperament. But how can we know which way our child should go, and what effect can we have on this inborn temperament?

Over the past thirty years, researchers in child development have been increasingly aware of how the quality and quantity of mothering and fathering can affect a child's temperament. The "goodness of fit" principle describes one of the most powerful influences on a baby's temperament. This principle states that how a baby fits into her care giving environment will positively or negatively affect the development of her personality.

While in the womb, the pre-born baby fits perfectly into her environment. Perhaps there will never be another environment in which the baby fits so harmoniously, an environment in which the baby's needs are automatically and predictably met. The womb environment is physically and emotionally very well organized.

Birth suddenly disrupts this organization. During the months following birth, the baby tries to regain a sense of organization. Birth and adaptation to post-natal life bring out the temperament of a baby, since for the first time she must do something to have her needs met. She is forced to act, to "behave." She must make an effort to get the things she needs in her care-giving environment. If hungry, she cries. If her needs are simple and she can get what she needs easily, she is labeled an "easy baby;" she fits. If a baby does not adapt readily to what is expected of her, she is labeled a difficult baby. She doesn't easily fit. Some babies fit easily into their environment, others do not.

The Need Level Concept

We believe that babies come wired with a certain temperament for a reason. Every baby possesses a certain level of needs which must be filled if she is to develop to her maximum potential, i.e., if she is to "go the way she should go." It stands to reason that an infant would also come wired with the temperament to communicate these needs.

The early language cues of a baby are a language of need. They are referred to as attachment-promoting behaviors, the most noteworthy of which is the infant's cry. An infant with a high level of needs also comes programmed with an intense way of communicating these needs. For example, babies who need a lot of holding in order to thrive will protest if they are put down.

Some babies are labeled as easy babies. They are content in a variety of care-giving circumstances. They don't cry much because their needs are easily met. They are somewhat consistent and predictable in their needs and adapt easily to a variety of schedules and parenting styles. (These are the babies everyone else has!)

Other babies, labeled difficult babies, may be supersensitive to changes in their environment. These babies have intense needs and voice equally intense protests when those needs are not met. Their mothers may say things like, "I just can't put her down," or "She wants to nurse all the time." These babies understandably receive the label "demanding," but we prefer to call them "high-need" babies.

We wish parents to view the demanding quality of their baby as a positive character trait that has survival benefits. If the baby were endowed with high needs, yet lacked the ability to communicate these needs, her survival would be threatened. This baby would not develop to her full potential.

The most common example of demanding behavior in a high-need baby is the baby who cries whenever she is put down. Before birth, a baby had a sense of oneness with the mother. After birth, the mother knows that the baby is now a separate person, but the baby does not feel separate. The baby still needs a sense of oneness with the mother, birth having changed only the manner in which this oneness is expressed. This baby will protest or fuss if her attachment to mother is disrupted. She needs to continue the attachment a bit longer, and fortunately she has the ability to demand this. If the baby's needs are heard and filled, she fits; she is in harmony with her environment. She feels right. When a baby feels right, her temperament becomes more organized and she becomes a "better" baby.

What happens if a baby's needs remain unfilled because her demands have gone unheard? A need which is not filled never completely goes away, but results in inner stress which sooner or later manifests itself as undesirable behavior, for example, anger, aggression, withdrawal or rejection. This baby does not feel right and therefore does not act right. A baby who does not act right is less of a joy to the parent, and baby and parents drift farther and farther apart. The parent becomes less adept at care giving and the baby becomes less motivated to signal her needs. The entire parent-child relationship operates at a lower level.

The need level concept leads us to a very important point that we wish new parents to fully understand: *Your baby fusses primarily because of her own temperament and not because of your parenting abilities.* Babies fuss because they *have to* in order to fit. However, the responsiveness of the care-giving environment does play a part in determining whether or not the baby's demanding temperament is channeled into desirable or undesirable personality traits.

Temperament Combinations
The temperament of the baby greatly affects the care-giving behavior of the parents. We realized this one day when a mother confided to us, "Our baby absolutely brings out

the best and the worst in me." Current research shows that the infant is not, as previously thought, a passive player in the parenting game, but rather an active participant in shaping the parent's behavior so that they can both fit into a style of parenting that brings out the best in each other.

There are two variables which lead to a good match, or fit, between mother and baby: the attachment-promoting or communicating skills of the baby and the responsiveness or sensitivity of the mother. Here are five of the most common examples of temperament matching and their outcome:

1. *An easy baby with a responsive mother.* This is a combination that will result in a good fit. Because mothers tend to feel that the "goodness" of their babies reflects their effectiveness as mothers, the mother in this case is likely to be delighted with the fit. Because easy babies are less demanding, they do not always initiate interactions with their care givers. But a responsive mother makes up for this by taking great care to initiate interactions with her baby.

2. *An easy baby with a more restrained mother.* This may not be as good a fit. Because the easy baby is not very demanding, a less responsive mother may expend relatively little effort in developing her mothering skills. She may feel that the baby doesn't seem to need her much and may seek more challenging activities elsewhere. In this match, not only does the mother fail to bring out the best in the baby, but the baby also does not bring out the best in the mother.

3. *A high-need baby with good attachment-promoting behaviors coupled with a responsive mother.* Each is likely to bring out the best in the other. The baby has high needs and has a corresponding temperament to communicate these needs. Mother, because she is open and responsive to the baby, develops a higher level of mothering skills to meet the needs of her baby. Even when the mother is confused at not being able to easily identify her baby's needs, she experiments with different responses until she finds one that works. Mother learns to nurture better and baby learns to communicate better, and the entire mother-infant relationship operates at a higher level.

Because the baby receives the consistent and predictable nurturing response that she needs, the baby learns to trust and refines her ability to communicate her needs. This makes it easier for mother to identify her needs and to comfort her. Baby and mother become mutually sensitive to each other. Because mother is able to listen better, baby learns to cry better, and the pair continually work to bring out the best in one another.

4. *A high-need baby with poor attachment-promoting skills and a responsive mother.* These babies, often known as "non-cuddlers," are slow to warm up to care giving. They appear not to need a lot of nurturing, but in reality they do. These babies may appear to be easy babies, but in reality are high-need babies in easy baby disguise. Parenting these babies may be difficult initially, because parents do not receive the feedback of appreciation they would get from a more cuddly baby who obviously enjoys being held and cared for. With a responsive mother, this type of baby usually does well. The mother does her best to initiate interaction and help the baby develop better attachment-promoting skills. These babies need the best responses a parent can give in order for the best in themselves to develop.

5. *A high-need baby and a restrained care giver.* This pair is at the highest risk for not developing a good fit. Neither one brings out the best in the other because the baby's language and needs are not understood. In this situation the baby may be endowed with good attachment-promoting skills, but because the mother does not develop her nurturing skills, the baby does not refine need-communicating skills.

In our experience, Christian parents are particularly vulnerable to this temperament mismatch. This is because of an unfortunate mindset which teaches new parents to be afraid to listen to their baby out of fear of being manipulated or losing their authority. Grandparents or friends may lead vulnerable new parents to feel that they are being poor disciplinarians if they give consistent nurturant responses to their baby. This quickly becomes a no-win situation. The parents lose the chance to develop their God-given intuitive nurturing skills due to their fear of listening and responding to their baby. The baby loses the opportunity to develop better communicating skills and refine some rough edges in her temperament.

Dr. James Dobson and other authors who write about the strong-willed child have stressed that these children, if not disciplined, are at high risk for behavioral problems later on. They also show character strengths which can be a blessing to themselves and their parents. While it is very important not to judge the type of person the high-need child will later become, by providing a nurturing care-giving environment we can mellow out the undesirable behavior traits in these children and decrease the risk of later behavior problems.

BILL: Babies don't come with directions, but if they did, Hayden's would have been written in a foreign language. Hayden, our fourth baby, was one of those children who expect every ounce of energy from both parents. She wanted to be held, nursed, and comforted constantly. Because she was content only when held, Martha and I were always playing "pass the baby." Hayden was in our arms by day and in our bed at night. She craved skin-to-skin contact and often fell asleep on my fuzzy chest when her mother had already given out.

Like all babies, Hayden had a special language of needy cries, and we had ears and hearts that listened and responded. She snuggled against our bodies in a baby carrier rather than being wheeled in a stroller. She could not be left in a church nursery, as our other babies had. We would take her with us into the church service, but during particularly high-need periods, Martha and I would take turns; one would be in church while the other walked Hayden around the church grounds.

Most of our friends prayed for us and supported our realization that we had a special baby. Other well-meaning advisers suggested that we let her cry in the church nursery so that she would "get used" to being left.

Somehow we all managed to bring out the best in each other. Hayden thrived during that first year, and Martha and I . . . survived. Yet something beautifully right was happening to me. Very subtly and gradually I was changing. After a year of feeling that I been doing nothing but giving, I realized I had received much in return. Hayden was teaching me how to nurture.

Survival Tips for Parents of High-Need Babies

High-need babies receive a variety of labels: colicky, fussy, demanding, exhausting. Because high-need babies need a higher level of parenting, it is important to recognize the high-need child early. You can often spot this baby even as a newborn, as if at birth she looks up at you and says, "Hi, Mom and Dad. You have been blessed with an above average baby, and I need above average parenting. If you give it to me, we're going to get along fine; if you don't, we're going to have a bit of trouble along the way."

Parents of high-need babies describe their children like this: extremely sensitive, intense, hyperactive, draining, unpredictable, unsatisfied, uncuddly, demanding. They wake frequently, want to nurse all the time, and can't be put down. These babies are usually very sensitive to changes in their environment. They do not have the capability of selectively filtering out disturbing stimuli in their environment. They cannot comfort themselves and must rely on their care givers for support.

Through ten years of studying these babies and through our own experience with Hayden, we have learned the following practical survival tips.

1. *Pray for support.* If you remain in harmony with God, you have a greater assurance of remaining in harmony with your high-need child. The following are some scriptural passages which we call how-to-cope verses.

"Apart from me you can do nothing." (John 15:5)

"Trust in the Lord with all your heart and lean not on your own understanding." (Proverbs 3:5)

"But those who hope in the Lord will renew their strength. They will soar on wings like eagles; they will run and not grow weary, they will walk and not be faint." (Isaiah 40:31)

"Give thanks in all circumstances, for this is God's will for you in Christ Jesus." (I Thessalonians 5:18)

"Do not be anxious about anything, but in everything, by prayer and petition, with thanksgiving, present your requests to God." (Philippians 4:6)

"I can do everything through him who gives me strength." (Philippians 4:13)

"Cast all your anxiety on him because he cares for you." (I Peter 5:7)

2. *Don't feel guilty.* "What am I doing wrong?" many mothers ask us. A fussy baby can absolutely shake the confidence of a new mother and destroy many of the rewarding aspects of parenting. Remember, moms, the "goodness" of your baby is not a measure of your effectiveness as a mother. Babies fuss because of their own temperaments, not because of your mothering abilities. The less confident you become, the less you are able to comfort your baby and the more inconsolable your baby becomes. This cycle often results in escape mothering rather than attachment mothering.

3. *Don't compare babies.* A mother of a high-need baby once said to us, "Why can't I handle my baby? Other mothers seem to be more in control of their babies. They can leave them and get other things done; I can't."

We advised this mother not to compare her baby with other babies or herself with other mothers. Keep in mind that mothers tend to exaggerate the "goodness" of their babies. Comparing babies will add nothing to your own relationship and contributes to your frustration and impending burnout.

Keep in mind God's "law of supply and demand:" God will supply you with the level of energy to meet the demands of your baby, providing you practice the style of parenting that allows this to happen.

Occasionally a family may have a fussy baby and parents with a low fussy tolerance. This is a high-risk situation, but through prayer and practicing the survival tips mentioned in this section, these parents will be able to increase their level of acceptance and keep the law of supply and demand in balance.

4. *Get dad involved.* One of the most common statements from mothers who have successfully coped with their high-need babies is, "I could not have survived without the support of my husband." High-need babies require shared parenting. These babies are continuously "in arms" babies, but mothers' arms occasionally wear out. In cultures which have the luxury of the extended family, the fussy baby is passed from arms to arms to arms.

High-need babies can be a severe strain on the marriage if shared parenting is not done. Fathers, keep in mind that mothers (especially the most committed mothers) are not noted for their wisdom in knowing when to call for help or recognizing that they are giving out. Be tuned in and sensitive enough to know when to step in and say, "I'll take over; you go do something just for yourself."

BILL: *Through dealing with our high-need daughter Hayden, I continued to grow in paternal sensitivity. I became sensitive to all my children, and this sensitivity carried over into our marriage. Even our sex life improved. My wife became more sensitive to me as a mate. (Nothing turns a woman on more than a man who is a sensitive and caring father.)*

Because Hayden was naturally closer to Martha than to me, I began to respect the phenomenon of mother-infant attachment. I didn't feel left out of the inner circle of mother and baby; I knew that somehow I was part of it, too, but in a different way. Hayden didn't love Martha more than me or less than me. She loved me differently.

Because I was around the house more and actively involved, our family life became more organized. I could provide a framework around which family members

*could grow and develop according to their potential. My
previous selfishness was giving way to sensitivity. Because my sensitivity filtered down, everyone became more
sensitive to one another. My investment was beginning
to pay off. I was getting hooked on fathering.*

5. *Group therapy.* Surround yourself with positive friends
and support groups. There is great consolation in knowing
that your baby is not the only baby in the whole wide world
that fusses.

It helps to seek advice and gentling tips from parents
who have recently coped with a high-need baby. In our
practice we keep a list of such parents and we often refer
new parents of a fussy baby to someone on our list. After
meeting with parents who truly do have a high-need baby,
the new parents often report, "We don't have a fussy baby
after all."

6. *Gentling tips.* Stillness and quietness is a state in which
many babies seem most relaxed. In the case of high-need
babies, motion and sound is their natural state. Most fussy
babies are calmed by three actions: motion, sound, and
physical contact—a back-to-the-womb type of environment.
In fact, one surviving mother of a high-need baby related
that it had helped her cope by regarding her pregnancy as
lasting eighteen months—nine months inside and nine
months outside! The art of gentling the fussy baby consists
of determining what motion, sound, and physical contact
your baby likes and needs, and how much you can give of
yourself without exhausting your parental resources. (You
will find more help in Chapter 8, "Wearing Your Baby.")

7. *Relax yourself.* A fussy baby can absolutely shatter the
nerves of even the most shatter-proof mother. Being held in
tense arms may be very upsetting to a baby who is already
very sensitive to tense vibrations. Here are some relaxation
tips to help you and your baby enjoy each other: take a warm
bath together; lie down and nurse your baby, tummy to
tummy, snuggled in your arms and breasts; get outdoor
exercise, even if you have to force yourself to do so.

Nap when your baby naps. Oftentimes mothers use the
baby's nap time to "get something done." High-need babies

seem to carry their waking personalities into their sleep patterns and are notoriously resistant to any attempts to schedule their sleep. They often can sleep only if someone rocks them and holds them the whole time and will wake up unless someone lies down with them and stays there through the whole nap. Don't feel that you are getting nothing done when you take a lot of naps with your baby. You are getting something done—mothering.

8. *Set priorities.* Most mothers of high-need babies become exhausted not so much because of their baby, but because they have tried to continue all of the outside activities and obligations they had before their baby arrived. You can't be all things to all people. If you have been blessed with a high-need baby, many of your previous commitments may have to be temporarily shelved. Your baby is a baby for a very short time.

Leaving the High-Need Baby
Because of the oneness that develops between a high-need baby and her mother, the pair may seem inseparable for the first year or two. Babies do not want to separate from the mother or the mother from the baby. It is important for a new mother of a high-need baby not to feel isolated or feel that she must stay home all the time. "Home" to a tiny baby is where the mother is.

Perhaps the most common problem Christian mothers face is their ambivalent feelings about leaving their new baby in the church nursery while attending service. One part of the mother's inner desire is to rejoin the fellowship and the church service; however, another part of her maternal instinct makes her feel uncomfortable leaving her baby. It is vital that you take good spiritual care of yourself so that you can take better maternal care of your baby. For this reason it is important that new mothers not feel ostracized from their Christian fellowship simply because they've just had a baby, especially a high-need baby.

Churches are beginning to recognize this dilemma by making mothers feel welcome to keep their babies with them during the service and offer them the option of a nursery with nurturing care givers so that mothers may feel more comfortable leaving their baby in the church nursery. Be sure to leave instructions with the nursery care giver that you wish to be called if your baby needs comforting. To worship or to mother should not be an either/or choice. A true Christian fellowship can provide a setting in which the mother is encouraged to do both.

MARTHA: *Hayden wasn't left with sitters much because she tolerated separation poorly. She wasn't left in the church nursery alone until she was ready. My ministry in the church became being available in the nursery to help other little ones, because I was there with Hayden when she was too old to sit still and nurse in church.*

We even kept her with us in Sunday school by learning how to keep her quietly busy so we could attend to the teaching and minimize the amount of distraction she might have caused. When she was three and a half she was eager, at last, to go off to her own Sunday school class, and she never looked back once.

Whatever the temperament of your baby, keep in mind that the greater the investment, the greater the return. By following the style of parenting that God has designed for you and your individual baby, you are likely to see a rich payoff in years to come when you realize how your baby and your parenting style have brought out the best in all members of the family.

CHAPTER SIX

Feeding Your Baby According to God's Design

Proper nutrition, or the lack of it, can have a profound effect on your baby's growth and development. Good feeding techniques can have a profound effect on your role as parents as well, since during the first year you will spend more time feeding your baby than in any other parent-baby interaction.

When a woman chooses to breastfeed her baby, she is guaranteeing him the best nourishment and the best nurturing by tapping into a God-given formula for mothering and feeding as old as creation. We see in Scripture an important message about nursing: it is not only for nutrition but for comfort. "You will nurse . . . and be satisfied by her comforting breasts" (Isaiah 66:11).

Let's examine the uniqueness of this divine design for infant nutrition.

God's Perfect Design for Infant Nutrition

God has designed that all species of mammals produce a nutrient that is uniquely formulated for the growth and development of the young of that species. We call this nutrient "milk." To appreciate the beauty of God's nutritional design, let's look at several species of mammals.

Cold-water mammals produce a milk high in fat, because these animals need high body fat to survive in their cold environment. The milk of range animals, on the other hand, is high in minerals and protein, because rapid bone and muscle growth is necessary to get a calf up and running shortly after birth to insure its survival. What is the survival organ of the human? The brain. And scientists have recently discovered components of human milk that are uniquely formulated to promote brain growth.

Unlike artificial formula, human milk is not static; it changes as the needs of your infant change.

1. *Your milk protects your baby.* The first milk your baby receives shortly after birth is called *colostrum*. Colostrum may be considered your baby's first immunization, as it is very high in immunoglobulins—germ-fighting elements. During pregnancy, your infant received a large supply of these immunoglobulins which crossed the placenta. Since a newborn is particularly vulnerable to germs, God has designed human milk to be most protective when a baby needs it most. The immunoglobulins which your baby received before birth are all used up between six months and a year, at which time an infant can manufacture his own immunoglobulins. As the maternal immunoglobulins are being used up during the first six months, you refuel this protective process by giving your baby the immuno-globulins in your milk.

In some cultures human milk is also known as "white blood" because it contains the same living white cells that blood contains. These white cells in your milk protect the baby against the germs that enter baby's immature intestines. They produce a special protein called immunoglob-ulin A, which acts like a protective paint, coating your baby's intestines and preventing the passage of harmful germs from the intestines into his bloodstream. Your baby needs a large supply of these immunoglobulins in his gut. If a new germ enters a mother's intestines, she produces antibodies to this germ. These antibodies are delivered to the infant through the mother's milk, protecting him from the same germ.

2. *Your milk helps your baby grow.* Human milk contains the amino acid taurine which promotes brain growth. Human milk also contains a special growth factor which stimulates DNA (the genetic building blocks within each cell), promoting cellular growth. Human milk is richer in the essential fatty acids uniquely formulated for human brain growth.

3. *Your milk provides optimal nutrition* which changes to meet the changing nutrient needs of your baby. All milk contains the proper balance (for that species) of the following nutrients: fat, carbohydrates, protein, minerals, iron, and vitamins.

Fats. In the first six months your infant grows faster than at any other time in his life, at least doubling his birth weight by six months. This is the time that baby needs milk highest in calories, and this is exactly what he gets. In the first six months the fat content in your milk is around four percent, like whole cow's milk. During the latter half of the first year, the fat content of your milk gradually lessens, becoming more like low-fat or two percent milk, because your baby needs fewer calories per pound of body weight as he grows. The hungrier your baby is, the higher the fat content of your milk becomes. If your baby is only thirsty, he will suck in a way that he receives the thinner fore-milk which is lower in fat content. If baby is hungry, he will suck in a way to receive the more creamy hind-milk which is higher in fat content and calories. Your milk has a higher fat content in the morning because your baby is usually hungrier in the morning.

Human milk, unlike pasteurized cow's milk or formula, contains enzymes which aid in fat digestion. The infant's immature intestines are deficient in these enzymes. Human milk fat is almost completely digested and absorbed, whereas some of the fat in cow's milk and formula is not digested and contributes to unpleasant stools. The lower fat content and the difference in sugars and bacteria in the stools of a breastfed baby account for the sweeter smell.

Carbohydrates. Because it contains more lactose, human milk is definitely sweeter than cow's milk, and the newborn taste is sensitive to this natural sweetness. To make formula attractive to infants, cane sugar or corn syrup is added. But it is important for parents to know that all sugars are not the same. Lactose (the sugar found in human milk) is a natural sugar for human infants, whereas cane or corn sugar may produce unnatural blood sugar swings and accompanying mood swings. This phenomenon is well recognized in older children, but it is possible that it also occurs in infants. Human milk contains the enzyme *lactase* which, together with baby's intestinal enzymes, helps digest lactose. Formula does not contain lactase. Lactose also favors a development of certain protective bacteria in the intestines. These bacteria fight off harmful bacteria that cause diarrhea.

Protein. Human milk protein is suited to human infants in a number of ways. The curd produced is smaller and more digestible than that of cow's milk. This is because the amount of protein, or *casein*, in cow's milk is four times that of human milk (cows grow four times faster than humans). The high casein content of cow's milk protein forms a heavy curd which is less digestible and contributes to gas formation, constipation, and "sore bottoms." The decreased digestibility of formula as compared to human milk is one of the reasons why formula-fed babies tend to remain "full" longer than the breastfed baby.

Minerals. The lower calcium and phosphorus content of human milk is better suited to the rate of bone growth of the human infant, which is slower than that of a calf. The lower amount of salt and mineral content in human milk is easier on the immature kidneys of a young infant.

Iron. The iron of human milk is uniquely formulated to meet the high iron requirements of the growing infant during the first year. The iron in your milk is at least fifty percent absorbed into your infant's blood, whereas the artificial iron that is added to formulas and cereals may be only ten percent absorbed, and the excess may interfere with the growth of normal bacteria within the gut. The reason for the improved iron absorption of human milk is a special protein in your milk called *lactoferin* that attaches to the iron in your milk and makes it better absorbed. The higher iron content accounts for the green color of a formula-fed baby's stool.

Vitamins. The milk of a well-nourished mother contains all the vitamins necessary for your infant.

Reasons for Unsuccessful Breastfeeding

Even though breastfeeding is a natural and God-given experience, some mothers do experience difficulty.

> MARTHA: *As a certified lactation consultant, director of a breastfeeding clinic, and a mother who has joyfully logged over fifteen years of breastfeeding our seven children, I have come to the conclusion that most of the so called "breastfeeding failures" could have been successes, had those mothers received the support, encouragement, and wise counsel of other women who understood God's design for the breastfeeding relationship.*

In our experience at the Breastfeeding Center, we have encountered the following reasons why some mothers try breastfeeding and fail, often through no fault of their own.

1. *A traumatic labor and delivery.* Some women are unable to breastfeed because of a medical complication separating mother and baby at birth. A mother recovering from a cesarean section may need most of her energy to heal herself and not have enough energy left to breastfeed. Lactation consultants trained to assist C-section mothers and mothers of premature babies can help in such situations.

2. *Being separated from baby, feeding on schedule instead of on cue, and not rooming in with baby are common reasons why breastfeeding doesn't work.* Rooming-in lessens the incidence of unsuccessful breastfeeding.

3. *Improper position and latch-on is, in our experience, the most common cause of not enjoying breastfeeding.* In our practice, every first-time mother spends at least an hour with a

lactation specialist during the first few days after birth. Baby learns to latch on properly before he develops wrong sucking habits.

Unsuccessful breastfeeding is not a fault of the design or the Designer. It is often due to someone tampering with this beautiful design.

Questions about Breastfeeding

Here are answers to some of the most frequently asked questions about breastfeeding.

▍ *How often and how long should I feed my baby?*

Early in your breastfeeding relationship you will realize that the term *schedule* has absolutely no meaning in breastfeeding a baby. The only schedule your baby will have, and should have, is his own. Breastfeeding is more than a mathematical exercise. One nursing mother put it this way, "I don't count the number of feedings any more than I count the number of kisses." Listen to your baby's cues and watch your baby, not the clock.

In the first few days most babies suckle in varying intensities, intermittently, and for long periods of time, even as long as an hour. Baby will often fall asleep during a feeding and then wake up in an hour and want to feed again. Realistically, expect your baby to breastfeed every two to three hours around the clock for the first month or two. The duration of the feeding often depends upon baby's sucking style.

▍ *How do I know that my baby is getting enough milk?*

In the first few weeks, it is not always easy to tell that your baby is getting enough milk, especially if you are a first-time mother. Here are some signs to help you know:

1. Your baby will have wet diapers often, at least six to eight wet cloth diapers (four to five disposable diapers) and two or more bowel movements per day.

2. Your breasts will feel full before feedings, less full after feedings, and leak between feedings.

3. If you feel your baby sucking vigorously, hear him swallowing, feel your milk-ejection reflex, and then see your baby drift contentedly off to sleep, chances are he has gotten enough milk.

I *Why does my baby want to nurse all the time?*

In the first few months, babies have "frequency days" when all they want to do is nurse. Here are some survival tips.

1. During high-need days, temporarily shelve all outside commitments that drain your energy. Your baby is a baby for a very short time, and no one's life is going to be affected if the housework isn't done on time. In our experience, mothers become burned out not so much because of the demands of their babies, but because of too many other commitments.

2. Be sure your baby is getting mostly milk at each feeding and not a lot of air. Effective burping techniques require placing firm pressure on your baby's tummy. Lean baby's weight against the heel of your hand as he sits on your lap, or drape him way over your should or over one knee, and firmly pat or rub baby's back.

3. Get used to wearing your baby in a sling or front carrier (see Chapter 8). This not only makes nursing more accessible, but it may be that your high-need baby is not always wanting to nurse, but is seeking the comfort of your closeness.

4. Avoid the "filler food" fallacy. You may be advised to give your baby a supplemental bottle or cereal with the implication that you don't have enough milk. This is not usually necessary. Your baby is simply signaling that he needs to nurse more, and you need to increase your level of supply to meet his level of need. If your baby is gaining weight poorly, you need to see a lactation consultant.

5. Sleep when your baby sleeps and don't be tempted to "get something done." You need to recharge your own system to cope with these high-need periods.

I'm a tense person. How can I relax better during nursing?

Create a relaxing atmosphere by developing a "nursing station." This is an area in your home especially set up for the nursing pair. It includes your favorite chair (preferably an armchair or rocking chair with arms at a comfortable height to support your arms while holding baby), plenty of pillows, a footstool, soothing music, a relaxing book, nutritious nibbles, and a supply of juice or water. Take the phone off the hook (or have it right next to you). This is like a nest within your home to which you can retreat with your baby, so you can more easily give him the quality and quantity of time he needs.

If you have a toddler who still needs a lot of attention, set up your station on a pad or mattress on the floor with special time-out activities for the older child such as snacks, music, books, and toys. This gives him access to you and reassures him that he is still important. Consider doing this in his room, where you can keep an eye on him.

How can my husband help in breastfeeding?

Many fathers feel left out of this inner circle of the breast-feeding pair. But in our survey of factors contributing to successful breastfeeding, a sensitive and supportive father was high on the list. One father in a successful breastfeeding family summed it up very wisely. "I can't breastfeed our baby, but I can create an environment which helps my wife breastfeed better." Fathers can bathe with, walk with, play with, and help with baby (changing, burping, soothing, etc.). Breastfeeding is indeed a family affair.

Advantages of Breastfeeding to Mother

The breastfeeding experience is a prime example of the mutual giving that occurs when a mother practices attachment parenting. As your baby sucks from your breast, a hormone called *prolactin* is released into your bloodstream. This hormone, perhaps the biological basis of the term "mother's intuition," is a special substance which travels throughout the internal highways of mother's body and "tells her which turn to take." In a very real sense, then, the baby gives to the mother the very hormone which helps her to mother him.

We have often referred to prolactin as the "perseverance hormone" that helps mothers get through those trying times. Prolactin relaxes mothers. Perhaps this hormone also accounts for the lower incidence of postpartum depression in breastfeeding mothers.

Recent studies have shown that the chance of breast cancer is much less in a breastfeeding mother, and incidence of breast cancer is lowest in those mothers who breastfeed for at least two years.

MARTHA: Breastfeeding has given me a sense of accomplishment on three levels: physical, mental, and emotional. Physically there is the pride in my ability to nourish my babies. I look at my three or six or nine month old and realize the beauty of the design that has allowed me to provide his total nourishment from my body. It is a real boost to be so completely a part of God's work in the growth and development of my child. Even more compelling is the realization that I have taught this baby how to feel, taste, see, smell, and hear using my own body as the source and the focus.

Home base is always the best teacher, allowing the baby to go from the totally familiar to the new, unfamiliar, and sometimes frightening as he begins to learn about the great wide world beyond mother. Breastfeeding provides a wonderful laboratory for all this learning to take place.

For example, in the experience of taste, the baby is tasting his mother's sweet milk (sweeter than cow's milk or artificial formula). The Hebrew word for taste means "to perceive." When I read Psalm 34:8, "Taste and see that the Lord is good," or Psalm 119:103, "How sweet are your promises to my taste," I can't help but think of the sweetness of breast milk.

The Apostle Peter used this fact to encourage believers in their spiritual growth. "Like newborn babies, crave spiritual milk, so that by it you may grow up in your salvation, now that you have tasted that the Lord is good" (I Peter 2:2). How interesting that the Hebrew child was weaned when he would be old enough to remember the sweetness of his mother's milk (around the age of three), just at the time he was introduced to the study of the Pentateuch and the sweetness of the Word of God.

As the baby is developing physically and mentally, he is also developing emotionally at his mother's breast. The breastfeeding relationship teaches a baby how to love, trust, feel safe, feel good about himself, and enjoy the life God gave him. All of this learning is preparation for loving, trusting, and enjoying God, being loved by God, and feeling secure in His care. Psalm 71:6 says it so beautifully: "From birth I have relied on you; you brought me forth from my mother's womb. I will ever praise you."

All of this learning, of course, was achieved primarily because of my presence. By its very nature, breastfeeding demands the immediate presence of the mother for the baby. You can't "prop" a breast and walk off to get something done!

Breastfeeding ties mother and baby together—"tied down" is the negative term. I am a very busy, achievement-oriented person, and if it had not been for the discipline of breastfeeding, I would have been making choices that would have separated me from my babies. God knew there were mothers like me who would need biological anchors in order to be available enough for the babies He would give them. Because of breastfeeding, I got the message loud and clear that my babies needed me, not just any pair of arms.

I have been deeply affected by the experience of giving myself over to the full-time nurturing of my children. Breastfeeding is the vehicle by which I express that nurturing and the foundation on which I have built *a relationship with each one of my children. I know each of them uniquely because we interacted so intimately and intensely.*

Formula Feeding

While breastfeeding is the first choice for an infant, there are circumstances in which it is not possible. In such a case, remember that the term "nursing" means comforting and nourishing, whether by breast or bottle. You can still "nurse" your baby. Here are some suggestions on how you and your baby can upgrade bottle feeding.

1. *Selecting a formula.* Your doctor or health care professional will advise you which formula to feed your baby. Most formulas are made from cow's milk or soy products and modified to provide adequate nutrition for your baby. Infant formula is available in three forms, powdered, liquid concentrate, and ready-to-feed. The form you choose is largely a matter of economics and convenience.

Follow the directions on the container carefully when preparing formula. Add the specified amount of water, no more, no less. Select an orthodontic-type nipple which fits into your baby's mouth similarly to the breast. The nipple hole should be only large enough to allow formula to drip around one drop per second without shaking.

2. *Frequency of feeding.* Tiny babies have tiny tummies. Smaller, more frequent feedings are best, especially in the early months. Because formula is digested more slowly than breast milk, formula fed infants can usually go longer between feedings than breastfed babies and are easier to schedule. Feed your baby every three hours during the day and at night as needed. Even if you schedule feedings every three hours, you will want to be flexible if your baby is hungry sooner or sleeps a little longer.

As a general guide, offer your baby around two to two and a half ounces of formula per pound per day. For example, if your baby weighs ten pounds, he will take around twenty to twenty-five ounces (about two and a half ounces every three hours). In the early weeks, your baby may take less than this amount. It is wise to give him an extra bottle of plain water each day. (Breastfed babies do not need extra water.)

3. *More than a meal.* Feeding your baby is not just delivering milk; feedings also deliver emotional nourishment. Your baby should always feel that a person is feeding him, not just a bottle. Interact with your baby during the feeding. Touch and groom him. Hold your baby while you feed him, and hold the bottle as though it were coming from your body. Look into your baby's eyes during the feedings. Most babies, breast- and bottle-fed, feed better if you are quiet while they suck, but they enjoy social interaction during the pauses in the feedings. Eventually you will develop a sense of your baby's feeding rhythm.

Starting Solid Foods

Breast milk or commercial formula (or a combination of the two) contains all the essential nutrients your baby needs for the first four to six months. In addition to this, your baby may not be equipped to completely digest solid foods before this time. Not only is the upper end of baby's digestive tract (tongue and teeth) not designed for early solids, neither are the rest of his insides. The baby's immature intestines may allow potential allergens to seep into the bloodstream, thus increasing the risk of the child developing more food allergies. Teeth seldom appear much before six months.

At four to six months, many digestive enzymes seem to click in. The developing intestines become like filters to screen out the larger potentially allergenic proteins or digest them into smaller, less allergenic substances. Teeth begin to appear. And your baby may show signs of wanting solid food. (This may happen before he needs solid food for nutritional reasons.)

Some signs of solid food readiness are your baby's watching food in transit from your plate to your mouth or reaching for food from your plate. If your baby exhibits interest in this way, try this: place a finger full of mashed, very ripe banana on the tip of your baby's tongue. If the tongue goes in, accompanied by an approving smile, baby is ready; if the banana comes right back at you accompanied by a disapproving grimace, he is not! Early on, babies have a tongue-thrusting reflex, meaning the tongue will protrude outward when any foreign substance is placed on it. Around four months this tongue-thrust reflex diminishes, and mashed or strained foods can be introduced.

Start with solids which are closest to milk in taste and consistency, e.g., mashed bananas. Remember, your baby has to develop an entirely new feeding mechanism, from suck-swallow to tongue-mashing and swallowing. Around six months, babies begin to show two exciting developmental skills which make feeding much easier: the ability to sit up in a high chair or on your lap and the ability to pick up small morsels of food with fingers and thumb. Allow baby to feed himself; it's good for his fine motor development. Sharing the food with face and shirt is part of the game.

In case your baby may be intolerant or allergic to a certain food, space each new food about one week apart and keep a diary of which foods he may be allergic to. The usual signs of food allergy are bloating and gassiness, sandpaper-like rash on the face, runny nose, watery eyes, diarrhea, diaper rash, night waking, and generally cranky behavior.

Favorite starter foods include bananas, rice and barley cereal, applesauce, peaches, pears, carrots, squash, sweet potatoes, mashed potatoes, and avocados. Start with about one teaspoon of each new food. Remember that your initial goal is to introduce your baby to the new taste and texture of solids, not to fill him up. Gradually vary the texture and amount to fit the eating skills and appetite of your baby. Some like solids of thinner consistency and want a larger amount, some do better with thicker solids and smaller amounts.

Offer solids at a time of the day when your baby seems hungriest, the most bored, and/or you both need a change of pace. Mornings are usually the best time for offering solids to formula-fed infants, because you have the most time with your infant and usually don't have to worry about preparing a meal for the rest of the family. A breast-fed infant should be offered solids when your milk supply is lowest, usually toward the end of the day. Since infants have no concept of breakfast, lunch, and dinner, it really makes no difference when they receive what.

Talk to your baby during feeding. Talk about both food and procedure, so that he learns to relate the words with the type of food and the interaction soon to follow, e.g., "Do you want carrots . . . open your mouth!" as you gently approach his mouth with the spoon. Let baby watch your mouth open; he will mimic your facial expressions.

Observe "stop signs." Pursed lips, closed mouth, head turning away from the spoon are all signals that your baby doesn't want to eat right now. Don't force feed. You want your baby to develop a healthy attitude toward both the food and the feeding.

To a baby, eating is a developmental skill. The more the baby enjoys an experience, the more efficiently he will advance in that skill. Infant feeding not only provides fun and nutrition for the baby; it also allows parents to witness and enjoy their baby's rapidly developing hand skills. Remember, feeding is not just a nutritional necessity—it's a social interaction!

CHAPTER SEVEN

Weaning According to God's Design

One of the most insightful passages about weaning is found in Psalm 131:2: "But I have stilled and quieted my soul; Like a weaned child with its mother, like a weaned child is my soul within me." The psalmist equates his feeling from trusting the Lord with the feeling of peace and tranquility that a weaned child has from trusting its mother.

Langes Commentary on the Holy Scripture offers some beautiful thoughts on the meaning of this psalm: "As the weaned child no longer cries, frets, and longs for the breast, but lies still and is content because it is with its mother; so my soul is weaned from all discontented thoughts, from all fretful desires for earthly good, waiting in stillness upon God, finding its satisfaction in His presence, resting peacefully in His arms."

The Hebrew word for wean is *gamal*, which means "to ripen." This term implies a readiness. Weaning does not mean a loss or detachment from a relationship, but rather a passage from one relationship to another. When a child was weaned in Old Testament times, it was a festive occasion: "The child grew and was weaned, and on the day

Isaac was weaned Abraham held a great feast" (Genesis 21:8).

Weaning implies a smooth passage from the security and instruction from mother and father to security and instruction from God. A child must first learn trust and intimacy with earthly parents whom she can see and feel in order that she can build on this secure foundation and attain trust and intimacy with God. If a child is weaned from her parents before being filled with trust and intimacy, she is spiritually unready to develop a relationship with God.

Read the biblical account of Samuel's childhood in I Samuel 1:21-28: "When the man Elkanah went up with all his family to offer the annual sacrifice to the Lord and to fulfill his vow, Hannah did not go. She said to her husband, 'After the boy is weaned, I will take him and present him before the Lord, and he will live there always.'

" 'Do what seems best to you,' Elkanah her husband told her. 'Stay here until you have weaned him; only may the Lord make good His word.' So the woman stayed at home and nursed her son until she had weaned him.

"After he was weaned, she took the boy with her . . . to the house of the Lord. . . . And she said to [Eli], 'As surely as you live, my lord, I am the woman who stood here beside you praying to the Lord. I prayed for this child, and the Lord has granted me what I have asked of Him. So now I give him to the Lord. For his whole life he will be given over to the Lord.' "

Samuel was three years or possibly older when he was weaned and taken by his mother to the temple to live. We interpret Hannah's story as a beautiful example of God's design for weaning a child from his mother to his God— an early example of "attachment mothering!"

In the biblical context, the term weaning also implies "filling up a child" with whatever contributes to the child's well being. Think of all the verses in Scripture describing the things with which God fills us: love, joy, peace, comfort, knowledge, the Spirit. What a child must be "filled with" are the tools that will help her build other relationships— foremost, a relationship with God, but also relationships with other persons of significance in her world.

When Should a Child Be Weaned?

As we have stressed throughout this book, some babies have higher levels of needs than others. This is why one should not set an arbitrary time limit on weaning a child. If a mother and father have practiced the attachment style of parenting from birth, they will intuitively know when and at what pace to wean their child.

Some people may feel that late weaning of a child will create unhealthy dependence, put the child in control, and generally contribute to a "spoiled" child. Both experience and research have shown this not to be true.

Studies comparing groups of babies who were identified as securely attached to their mother with matched controls described as insecurely attached showed that the securely attached babies (those who were not weaned before their time) actually grew to be more independent, separated more easily from their mothers, moved into new relationships with more security and stability and were, in fact, easier to discipline.

Over the past ten years we have studied our own patients who were not weaned before their time and noticed the following qualities in these children: they are easier to discipline; they show less anger; their transition from one developmental stage to another is smoother and less anxious.

What happens to a child who is weaned before her time? We have noticed that children who have been prematurely weaned, i.e., "unfilled," exhibit what we call diseases of premature weaning: anger, aggression, more tantrum-like behavior, anxious attachment to care givers, and less ability to form deeper and more intimate relationships.

Even though you may feel secure in the pace in which you are weaning your child, be prepared for well-meaning advisers to shake your confidence a bit by saying, "What, you're still nursing!" The subtle accusation here is that you are creating an overdependency, that you are being possessive, that you are allowing your child to control you.

Possessiveness means keeping a child from doing what she needs to do because of some need you have. This is unhealthy and not in accordance with God's design. But by nursing your child as long as your child needs to nurse, you are meeting her needs and developing her trust in you. Have confidence in your mothering style, pray for guidance, and seek consultation from trusted, like-minded advisers. Natural weaning is a balance between the mother's willingness to release the baby and the baby's readiness to separate from the mother.

MARTHA: In my early days of parenting I was young, uninformed, and unconvinced of the importance of my personal presence for our babies. With each of our first three babies, I worked part-time. I thought I had to work, since my husband was a student and his income was about a third of what we needed to live on. Consequently, our first three children were weaned before their time. The first two boys were breastfed for eight months, the third, for seventeen months.

In retrospect, it's easy for me to see that I needed more involvement and commitment to breastfeeding— a breastfeeding support group such as La Leche League would have been a great help. I knew about La Leche League from my nurse's training, and I had read their book, The Womanly Art of Breastfeeding. *But I thought I knew all there was to know about breast-feeding and, since I had no difficulties, I didn't seek out any support. If I had, I would have been encouraged to think more carefully about going back to work, even part-time. In our situation, had we understood the importance of a mother's presence to our children, we would have dipped into the inheritance I had from my father. (What better way to use that money, than to allow a baby to have his mother full time?)*

La Leche League would also have taught me that early solids and early cup training are not necessarily in baby's best interest. I have pictures of me shoving cereal into a vehemently protesting two-week-old baby! Because he was eating solid food and drinking from a cup so well at eight months, he refused to breastfeed one day (after a trip to the emergency room to have stitches), and I took this to mean that he was ready to wean. He may have been ready physically, but emotionally neither one of us was ready.

This untimely weaning prepared the way for my next big mistake. We planned a long trip to Europe when Jim was sixteen months old, and because he was so independent of me (or so I thought), it simply didn't occur to us to take him along. Instead we chose to leave him with Bill's mother for—I have a hard time admitting this—four weeks. We will never know the effects of this temporary abandonment on our child, but we have earnestly prayed for God's healing as we have learned more about child development and have come to realize the harm that is done when a baby is left for longer than a few days with someone to whom he has no attachment.

The story gets worse. Our second baby was born twenty-six months after the first, and we moved to a new city (our third move in three years) for Bill's resident training. This baby was weaned also at eight months, even though I had no "reason" at all this time. I remember holding him on the night of his eight-month birthday and thinking as he nursed off to sleep, "This is the last time I'm going to breastfeed this baby." I remember feeling incredibly sad, but I had no one to talk to, to help me understand why. Again, La Leche League would have made a profound difference in my life.

Ignoring my maternal instincts caused me to misread my baby and myself. I became bored with motherhood and easily frustrated, struggling alone with dirty diapers and runny noses. I failed to see beyond to the joys, challenges, and fulfillment a professional mother could have. As I learned more about mothering, and more about God, I knew I had to be and wanted to be more available to my children. I am only sorry that it took me three babies to learn this lesson completely.

Steps in Weaning

The American Heritage Dictionary defines weaning this way: "To withhold mother's milk and substitute other nourishment." From this it seems that there are two phases in

91

weaning—detachment and substitution. As your baby is detached from the nutritional nourishment of your milk, and solid food is substituted for it, other forms of emotional nourishment should be substituted for the emotional detachment from your breast. Here are some tips:

1. *Try to breastfeed your infant for nutrition for at least one year.* The time of one year is an arbitrary figure, but it seems to be most in keeping with current medical teaching. In fact, most species of animals breastfeed their young until they triple their birth weight, which in human infants is around one year of age.

Between one and two years, weaning begins because a child has the physical abilities to separate from mother (e.g., walking). There seems to be a parallel between a child's motor abilities and her rate of weaning, in that from one to two years a child walks from mother, and from two to three years a child runs from mother. From one to two years a child has an interest and the fine motor abilities to take in alternative forms of nourishment, the ability to maneuver food with her hands, and the verbal ability to express her desires.

At this age, an important developmental ability kicks in which aids the toddler in weaning from mother—the development of object permanence. During the first nine to twelve months, a baby does not yet have the memory skills to imagine mother exists when she cannot see her. Between one and two years the toddler can develop a mental picture of mother even when she is in the other room; she, as it were, carries mother with her as she explores her environment. This cognitive ability facilitates weaning.

2. *Weaning should take place from person to person, not from person to thing.* As baby weans from mother's breast, another person should substitute other forms of nourishment, and this person naturally should be father.

3. *Wean gradually.* Weaning by desertion (leaving baby to go on a get-away holiday) is definitely to be avoided. Detachment from the mother's breast and detachment from the whole mother may be a combined stress that is

too much for baby to handle. The time-honored weaning method of "don't offer, don't refuse" seems to work the best for most mothers and babies. Between one and three years, as babies are naturally weaning into other relationships, they will periodically return to mother as their home base for nutritional and emotional refueling.

Be prepared for increases in nursing frequency as toddlers return to their secure home base during periods of high need or stress. Two year olds will often spend several months needing to nurse nearly as often as a newborn. While this will sometimes be perceived as a nuisance or an overdependency, it is a normal and healthy state of development as baby is returning to a known home base in order to be filled with a relationship she knows and from which she develops a comfortable feeling that it is now okay to proceed into less known relationships or more independent stages.

4. *Develop creative alternatives to breastfeeding.* After your infant has been nursing a year, this relationship is so beautifully fixed in her developing mind that some toddlers give absolutely no indication of slowing down their nursing frequency. Many mothers have told us, "She waits for me to sit down and then pounces."

The reason for this is the child's developing memory is like a big record; and she cuts grooves in this record. The nursing groove is probably one of the deepest your child will ever cut, and she therefore returns to this frequently until other grooves are cut in her memory record.

The age at which children willingly accept alternatives to breastfeeding is extremely variable. Expect nap nursing and night nursing to be the last breastfeeding relationship to wean. Many toddlers will retain their desire to breastfeed off to sleep well into the second and third year.

It is helpful to develop creative alternatives when your toddler is in need of comforting. If you only offer your breast as a solution, it will be harder for her to settle for anything else as she gets older. Toddlers may want to nurse when they are bored or need your attention, yet often a story or a romp in the backyard may be even closer to what the child wants.

Just be careful, though, because some children will try to have both a story and a nursing at the same time! If she figures out you can hold the book for her to see while she nurses, you'll never again be able to use, "How about a story instead?"

If the child really needs to nurse, she'll let you know. (It is always best to not refuse if a child insists, but then you can limit the time to what you feel you can give.)

MARTHA: One night my three year old was ready for bed, but I was feeling unable to both nurse her and read a story. I knew she could go to sleep just fine without breastfeeding when I was not available, so I gave her a choice between a story and a nursing. To my surprise, she chose the story. (I had been secretly hoping she would choose the nursing, because that actually took less time!)

When she was younger I had learned another approach to substituting one form of nourishment for another. I was newly pregnant and struggling with the discomforts of breastfeeding that result from ultra-sensitive nipples, one of the changes of pregnancy. I wanted to continue nursing her off to sleep, but found it impossible to give her the twenty minutes or so it took. So I limited her sucking to about three minutes, then let her snuggle close and rest her hand quietly on my breast. Just snuggling didn't do it—she needed the connection, the reassurance that "her" breasts were still there for her. In fact, she went to sleep immediately, giving me precious resting time.

As you develop more playful interactions as alternatives to breastfeeding, your child will gradually learn to be content with these alternative interactions as a substitute.

CHAPTER EIGHT

Wearing Your Baby

"You whom . . . I have carried since your birth. I have made you and I will carry you" (Isaiah 46: 3, 4). In Scripture, there are many references to God carrying His children, all giving a sense of peace and security. It is a wonderful picture, especially when you consider how mothers in biblical days transported their babies. They didn't have carriages, prams, or strollers. Instead they wrapped their babies around themselves, making slings out of their shawls. They wore their babies, as if the babies were part of their mothers' apparel.

Our personal interest in the art of baby wearing began several years ago while doing research and preparation for our book, *The Fussy Baby*. We noticed that the more babies were carried, the less they cried. Mothers with fussy babies would calmly say, "As long as I wear him, he's content!"

Based upon these observations, we began advising parents to carry their babies as much as possible right after coming home from the hospital. We told them to experiment with various baby carriers and choose the one most comfortable for themselves and their baby. To the mothers we said,

"Try to get used to wearing your baby in the carrier just as you would wear one of your favorite pieces of clothing."

Over a period of five years, we observed that mothers who carried their babies enjoyed greatly improved behavior in their babies. Carried infants cried much less, showed fewer colicky episodes, and in general, seemed more content. And when babies are content, parents are content.

Encouraged by the observations on our own patients, we searched medical literature to see what others had found. Infant development specialists whose writings we respect, such as Marshall Klaus and T. Barry Brazelton, noticed that babies in other cultures who are carried in a variety of homemade slings cry much less than their Western counterparts, who are "wheeled" rather than "worn."

A patient recently told us about a "ground touching ceremony" she witnessed on the Island of Bali, where babies are carried or worn for the first six months of life, being put down only to sleep next to the mother. At six months of age, the baby is ceremoniously put down on the ground to crawl and learn free-style movements.

New research is proving what experienced mothers have long known—that something good happens to parents and infants when they're physically attached. Infant development specialists have approached this problem in the following fashion, called a randomized-control trial. They studied two different groups of mother-infant pairs. One group, called the increased carrying group, were advised to carry their babies at least an extra three hours a day. The other group were given no specific instructions. The infants in the increased carrying group cried fifty percent less than the infants of the control group.

Other researchers have also noticed that carried infants show a higher level of visual alertness. It seems that carrying babies reduces crying by creating an environment which lessens the baby's *need* to cry.

The Benefits of Baby-wearing
Rediscovering the lost art of baby-wearing can have beneficial effects on your baby's development. It can also con-

tribute to your overall enjoyment of your baby in a number of ways.

Carrying settles the baby. Carrying seems to help settle babies by its effect on the vestibular system located behind each ear. This system is similar to three tiny carpenter's levels, one oriented for side-to-side balance, another for up-and-down, and the third for back-and-forth. They all function together to keep the body in balance. Every time you move, the fluid in these "levels" moves against tiny hair-like filaments which vibrate and send nerve impulses to the muscles in your body that will keep you in balance. For example, if you lean over too far to one side, the vestibular system signals that you should lean back to the other side to stay in balance.

While being carried, a baby moves in all three of these directions. The pre-born baby has a very sensitive vestibular system which is constantly stimulated, because the fetus is almost in continuous motion. Motion, not stillness, is the normal state for a baby. Carrying reminds baby of the womb.

Carrying regulates the baby. A newborn's movements are random and jerky. Most of the cues he gives his parents seem purposeless and hard to decode. His bodily functions are irregular, most noticeably in breathing patterns and heart rate. His day-night patterns are exhaustingly irregular and his feeding patterns notoriously unpredictable. In the early months, baby seems to waste a lot of energy fussing in order to adjust to life outside the womb. His behavior fluctuates, causing parents to exclaim, "One minute he's relaxed and quiet; the next he's tense and upset."

Much research attests to the value of the mother as a regulator of her baby. During baby-wearing, mother (or father) provides an external regulating system which balances the irregular tendencies of the baby. Picture how these regulating systems work.

Mother's rhythmic walk (which baby has been used to for nine months) reminds baby of the womb. This familiar rhythm, imprinted on baby's mind in the womb, now reappears in the "outside womb" and has a calming effect.

Mother's heartbeat, beautifully regular and familiar, reminds baby of the sounds of the womb. Mother's rhythmic respiration serves as another biological regulator as baby is placed tummy to tummy, chest to chest with mother.

Another way mother exerts this regulatory effect is by stimulating the regulating hormones in baby's developing adrenal and nervous systems. Researchers have shown that continued mother-infant attachment, such as baby-wearing provides, stimulates the infant to achieve quicker day-night regulation. Apparently mother's presence exerts a regulatory influence on baby's adrenal hormones, which promote night sleeping and day waking.

Mother's voice, which baby is constantly exposed to during baby-wearing, has been shown to regulate baby's limb movements. Video analysis of an infant's body movements while mother was talking showed her infant moved in perfect synchrony with the inflections of her speech during her unique "baby talk." The synchronous movements did not occur in response to a stranger's voice. In essence, the mother's rhythmic movements and vocalizations "teach" the baby to put more rhythm into her movements, balancing out the usual newborn tendency toward irregular, uncoordinated, and purposeless movements.

Carrying helps babies cry better. Besides lessening the amount of crying, baby-wearing lessens the intensity of baby's cries. By creating an organized, womb-like environment, wearing lessens a baby's need to cry. And when baby does cry, baby-wearing teaches him to "cry better." To understand how this is possible, let's review our analysis of the newborn's cry.

As discussed in Chapter 4, a baby's cry is a perfect signal, strong enough to draw the comforting care giver toward the baby, but not so intense as to provoke avoidance of the baby. The early phase is not an unpleasant sound and is easily extinguished once the baby is held and comforted. If this initial cry is unanswered, the cry intensifies into a shrill, ear piercing, disturbing sound which promotes avoidance in the care giver and anger in the baby.

Because a baby-wearing mother is so close to her infant, she anticipates baby's pre-cry signals and meets baby's needs even before baby has to cry. Both the baby and the mother learn non-crying modes of communication. Even if mother occasionally misses the opening cue, and baby does cry, because the pair is so close, the mother gives an immediate nurturant response, not requiring the cry to intensify. In effect, baby learns to cry better.

Mothers, please remember that it is not your fault that your baby cries, nor is it your job not to allow your baby to cry. The best that you can do is to create a secure environment that lessens baby's need to cry and not to let him cry alone.

BILL: Babies' cries are something for which I definitely have a low tolerance and, as a director of a newborn nursery, I was astonished at the disturbing cries of some newborns. Some babies have the good manners to start out with the attachment promoting cries which, if promptly attended to, don't escalate. Others click immediately into an ear piercing, shrill detachment cry. I would open the door of the nursery, hear one of those ear piercing cries, and want to shut the door and run.

These cries sometimes invoke anger rather than sympathy toward the baby. Nursery nurses quickly identify such babies, saying, "This one is going to be a handful." I began to wonder if we could identify babies with particularly disturbing cries and mellow out these cries during the first few weeks.

Jeffrey, the second born of an attached and committed mother, was the product of a very stressful labor and birth. Jeffrey's cry was shattering—even at delivery, it almost cleared the room. The nurses couldn't handle the sound and would quickly shuttle him into his mother's room. Susan, Jeffrey's mother, had more tolerance, but even she admitted that his cry was disturbing their bonding relationship.

As an experiment, we advised her and her husband to wear Jeffrey in a sling for at least four hours every day, more if possible. They were also instructed to tape record his cries over a period of two weeks. Within a week, Jeffrey's cry mellowed considerably, enabling his mother to enjoy being with him. "He cries much nicer now," she reported. Susan and her husband created a care-giving environment in which Jeffrey had no need to be angry and certainly no need to cry angrily.

In most of these "crybabies" we have studied, baby-wearing early in the newborn period not only lessened the *frequency* of crying but mellowed the *nature* of the cry into a more tolerable and attachment-promoting sound.

Carrying helps babies learn. If carried babies cry less, what do they do with their "free time"? They learn! Here is the reason: A baby who is carried more cries less, and therefore spends more time in the state of *quiet alertness* (also called interactive quiet). This is the behavioral state in which a baby is most receptive to learning from his environment. The behavioral state of quiet alertness gives the parents and baby a better opportunity to interact with each other. Also, researchers have reported that carrying enhances a baby's visual and auditory alertness.

One reason that baby-wearing enhances learning is that baby is intimately involved in the baby-wearer's world. The baby becomes accustomed to your bodily movements and sees things from your viewpoint. Baby sees what mother or father sees, hears what they hear and, in some cases, feels what they feel. A carried baby is more aware of his parent's face, walking rhythm, voice, and scent. Baby becomes aware of and learns from all the subtle facial expressions and other body language, voice inflections and tone, breath and emotion of the baby-wearer. Baby and mother, by their mutual sensitivity, share emotions. Baby-wearing mothers often report, "When I am happy, he's happy. When I am sad, he's sad. My baby seems to catch my spirit."

A parent will relate to the baby much more often just by virtue of the fact that baby is "sitting there right under my nose." Proximity increases interaction as baby constantly learns how to be human. Carried babies are intimately involved in their parents' world, because they participate in what mother and father are doing. It is important that babies be exposed to the parents' lifestyles in order to adapt to the culture into which they were born. In one culture, a mother may be working in the fields or weaving baskets; in another, she may be typing on a computer. In any case, babies worn during these activities are intimately exposed to and learn about the world of the adult—eventually to be the world of the child.

Carrying helps babies thrive. All babies grow, but not all babies thrive. Thriving means growing to one's fullest potential. We don't believe that there is any mysterious scientific reason why carried babies thrive more. If a baby wastes less energy crying, he has more energy left over to thrive. Researchers believe that during the state of quiet alertness, which baby-wearing promotes, all of the infant's physiological systems work better. In our practice we have used the therapeutic value of baby-wearing in babies who, for a variety of medical reasons, fail to thrive. We have noticed greatly enhanced growth and development even after a few weeks of baby-wearing.

Consider the alternative infant care practice, where baby is separate from the mother most of the day and is only picked up and interacted with at dutiful intervals. Life at a distance has no learning value. The voices baby may hear in another room are not associated with anything happening to him. Because they have no meaning to him, he gets the message that they are not important or worth storing.

Normal sounds of daily activities may either have learning value to the infant or disturb her. If a baby is alone, sounds may frighten him. If he is worn, these sounds have learning value. The mother filters out what she perceives as unsuitable for the baby and gives the infant an "it's okay" feeling when exposed to unfamiliar sounds and experiences.

Because baby is separate from her, mother does not, as a matter of course, gear her activities and interactions as if baby were a participating second or third party. At best, baby is involved in a spectator sport rather than as a participant in a contact sport. The baby-wearing mother, on the other hand, because she is used to her baby being with her, automatically gears her interactions to include the baby. The baby, in turn, feels that he is included and feels that he is valuable—a real boost to baby's emerging self esteem.

Baby-wearing fits in with our busy lifestyles. Many mothers who have part-time jobs outside the home have been able to wear their babies at work. Jobs such as selling real estate, shop keeping, demonstration of products, house cleaning, and many others lend themselves well to baby-wearing. Janice, a mother whose business involves cleaning homes a few hours a day, wears her baby in a sling while doing housework. A pediatrician friend of ours wears her baby in the office. Kathy, our office nurse, wears her new baby to work. Imagine what baby Elizabeth is learning! When mother answers the phone, baby answers the phone. When mother talks to people, baby hears the conversation. When mother is typing, baby sees and hears the typewriter. Baby is intimately a part of the action—a valuable learning experience for her.

Some employers are initially reluctant to permit mothers to wear their babies in the work environment, but we encourage them to give it a fair trial. Salespersons in baby shops and department stores often find baby-wearing to be a real plus for their credibility. Employers often find that baby-wearing mothers actually do a more productive job, since they so appreciate being given the opportunity to have their babies with them. They make an extra effort to prove that they can do two jobs at once. One retail employer found the baby to be an added attraction for his customers, who sensed that a centuries-old custom of working and wearing was being practiced.

MARTHA: I am a lactation consultant and teach breastfeeding classes. One day, just before one of my seminars, six-month old Matthew developed a fussy period. Not wishing to cancel my class, but more strongly not wanting to leave Matthew in a high-need period, I wore him in a sling while delivering a one-hour lecture to 150 pediatricians. After we (mother and contented baby) finished our talk on parenting styles, a doctor came up to me and exclaimed, "What you did made more of an impression than what you said!"

Carrying babies is good for fathers, too. The feeling that baby gets by being carried by father is not greater or less than that of being carried by mother, it is just different. It is this different style of stimulation that babies enjoy.

For example, babies enjoy the *neck nestle*, where baby's head is nestled into father's neck. In the neck nestle, father has a slight edge over mother. Tiny babies hear not only through their ears, but also through the vibrations of their skull bones. The vibration of the deeper male voice while father talks and sings, carrying the baby with head against father's voice box in front of his neck, will often lull the fussy baby back to sleep.

The *warm fuzzy* is another uniquely male variation of the snuggle hold during baby-wearing. Place baby's ear near your heart, bare skin to bare skin. The combination of the pulsing of your heartbeat and the movement of your chest, plus the rhythm of your walk, all introduce baby to the uniqueness of being worn by dad. If baby falls asleep during the warm fuzzy, lie down with him and drift off to sleep together.

For a father to be comfortable wearing his baby, and a baby to respond to dad's baby-wearing techniques, is a real bonus for mothers of high-need babies. Said one mom, "I love our new baby, but I found that I had to wear him constantly. I was burning out. My husband feels very insecure in calming fussy babies, so I was reluctant to release our baby to him during those trying fussy times.

"Baby wearing was the answer. After my husband became acclimated to wearing our baby in the baby sling, and I saw that the baby liked it, I felt more comfortable handing our baby to him. Initially I would hover over them to make sure our baby would stop fussing, but as soon as Jim proved himself as a competent baby-wearer, I felt a sense of great relief. Even though I wear our baby most of the time, having my husband share this experience gives me a much needed break."

> BILL: *As the father of seven and a certified baby-wearer, I feel that it is important that babies get used to their fathers, too.*
>
> *Mornings were my special time with our sixth child, Matthew. After nursing in bed, Matt was awake and aware and ready to begin the day—with me. Each morning we took a walk together to the bluff overlooking the ocean. Matthew soon grew to anticipate this early morning ritual. After waking and nursing he would roll over and look up at me as though to say, "Let's get going, Pop." As we'd walk, Matthew would nestle his head under my chin, mold his body to mine, and relax into the rhythm of my walk. Early morning is such a prime time for babies. Matthew's little mind seemed so alert, although at times I was still half asleep. Matthew may never remember these father-baby walks, but I will never forget them.*
>
> *I felt a real high the first time I put our latest baby, Stephen, in the neck nestle and snuggled him securely against my chest for a walk. As we strolled together, I felt a sense of wonderful completeness. Sometimes I wear him for hours at a time. I feel right when we are together and not completely fulfilled when we are apart—feelings usually reserved for the mother-infant pair. I'm glad to have a piece of this baby-wearing action, too!*

Fears of New Baby-wearers

Parents new to the idea of baby-wearing frequently ask us, "Does wearing your baby result in an overly dependent baby?" They are concerned about "spoiling" if they carry their baby so much. But in our experience and that of others, carried babies actually turn out to be more secure and more independent. Because they have grown up in early infancy with a secure home base, these infants seem to separate more easily and experience less separation anxiety.

Another common concern is this: "Does carrying diminish the baby's desire to crawl?" Carried babies do not show diminished development. In fact, carrying may actually enhance a baby's overall neurological development, probably because of the energy-sparing effect of reduced crying. There have been studies showing that carried and securely attached infants actually showed enhanced motor development over that of matched infants of the same age who were carried less and who were less securely attached. We believe that motion has a calming effect on the baby to the extent that the baby's neuromuscular system is then able to show more organized motor development.

We want to emphasize here that this style of carrying does not imply being restrictive or possessive in baby's development. Possessiveness means keeping the baby from doing what he needs to do because of some needs the parent has. As parents get more adept with this style of baby care, they will intuitively know when baby needs to be carried and when he needs to be put down.

"Wearing Down"
First-time parents may have been led to believe that the way babies go to sleep is that at some pre-assigned time you put your half-awake baby into the crib, pat him on the back, say "night-night," turn out the lights and leave the room. Baby peacefully drifts off to sleep without much bother. This only happens in books and movies or for everybody else's baby. Most babies want or need to be nursed down (meaning comforted to sleep in the care giver's arms).

Baby-wearing allows the infant to more easily make the transition from an awake state into sleep. When you feel that baby is ready to go to sleep (or you are ready for baby to go to sleep) wear your baby in the sling in the position you have found to be least stimulating and most sleep inducing. When your baby is in the state of deep sleep (recognized by a motionless face and limp limbs), lie down on your bed with baby still in the sling and gently slip yourself out of the sling. Allow baby to remain in the sling, using it as a cover.

Wearing down is particularly useful for the reluctant napper. Sometimes it helps to leave baby in the snuggle position on your chest while you both drift off to sleep together. This can be done during nap time on a floor, a couch or any place where baby and baby-wearer can comfortably get an hour's sleep.

"Wearing Out"

How often have you felt, "I'd love to go out, but I've just had a baby"? Some new mothers go stir-crazy after a few months. There is nothing in the mother-baby contract that says you have to stay home and become a recluse simply because you have a new baby. Nor is a new mother ready to leave her baby to go out. Baby-wearing allows you to "have your baby and take it with you."

MARTHA: *When our son Stephen was two months old, we were invited to a formal affair. Rather than decline the invitation, as new parents usually do, I wore Stephen in a fashionable sling and had a great time. Except for a few nursing snacks, Stephen settled peacefully in the sling during the three and a half hour affair. Not only was he not a disturbance, he was often the center of attention.*

Onlookers would initially have a puzzled expression on their faces, as if wondering, "What is that she's wearing?" The puzzlement turned to admiration, "Why, it's a baby! How cute!" By the end of the evening, as the guests noticed how content we were with our baby-wearing arrangement, there was an air of acceptance throughout the room. Baby-wearing had achieved not only social approval but social admiration.

Other Pluses of Baby-wearing

Carrying is part of safety and accident prevention. Having a baby in a protected yet interesting enclosure is especially valuable when visiting unfamiliar or unsafe environments filled with sharp edges or breakable objects. A sling can also serve as a shield to protect your baby's eyes from undesirable sights or inappropriate scenes or pictures that could frighten an impressionable young mind.

While infants enjoy being worn by their parents best, babies will adapt to substitute care givers better if worn in the sling they are used to. Brian, a toddler in our practice, called his sling "my little house." Home to a tiny baby is the sling, even if worn by a sitter.

When adults in the family wear their baby, they demonstrate to children that big people carry little people. Our own children and grandchildren are likely to adopt the style of parenting that they received or witnessed as children. For example, our seven- and eleven-year-old daughters, and sometimes our four-year-old son, will wear their dolls in homemade baby slings. This is because they have witnessed us wearing Stephen so often.

The effect of how role modeling affects children's view of the mother-infant relationship was brought home to us one day when six-year-old Hayden was asked to draw a mother and baby. She drew the two as essentially one person, because that was her concept of mothers and babies. She recognized that, at least in the early months, mothers wear babies, and the two are inseparable.

The "Up" Baby

A commitment to wearing babies means changing our mindset regarding what babies are really like. New parents may think of the picture-book baby as one who lies quietly in a crib, gazing passively at dangling mobiles. They may think that baby should be picked up to be comforted, fed, played with, and then put down; "up" periods are just dutifully intervals to quiet baby long enough to put him down again.

The concept of carrying reverses this view: babies are carried most of the time, and put down long enough for parents to attend to their own needs or during sleep time, and allowed floor freedom for those necessary free-style movements that babies love to do. "Down" babies learn to cry to get picked up. "Up" babies learn non-crying body language signaling their need to get down.

Some babies need more carrying than others. Certain babies, whom we call high-need babies, settle quite nicely when carried. These babies have a tendency to stiffen, arch, and seem to be doing continual back dives. These babies profit from the bending posture that carrying gives, and they enjoy the closeness of being wrapped around mother's or father's body. Some high-need babies, called "uncuddlers," protest being carried as if they find the cocoon-like environment of a carrier too restrictive. With patient practice and creative positioning (such as the facing forward position), even these babies often melt and mold into a cuddle posture and eventually adapt to a carrier.

The amount of carrying usually decreases as baby increases with age and motor skills. Yet, even the toddler may show occasional high-need periods when he needs increased carrying. In fact, carrying is especially beneficial during those toddler years when the whining toddler pulls incessantly at mother's skirt or father's pants, giving the pick-me-up cue. After all, the child wants to be part of the action, and the action is up where mom and dad are.

Choosing the Right Baby Carrier

Experiment with different carriers before purchasing one and look for these three main features: safety, comfort, and versatility.

1. *Safety.* Be sure the baby can be securely positioned in the carrier. Early on, as both parents and baby get used to an individual carrier, it is important to support the "package" with one or both arms. Choose a carrier that has been thoroughly tested by a reputable manufacturer. Although there are many baby carriers on the market, we feel that some of these have not been adequately safety-tested.

2. *Comfort—for both parents and baby.* Cotton (or a cotton-polyester blend) is the most comfortable and washable fabric. A well-designed carrier should distribute the baby's weight on the shoulders and hips of the adult, not on the back and neck. It should be well-padded over your shoulders and along your back, and wherever the edges of the carrier press against baby's torso and legs.

3. *Versatility.* To avoid having to purchase a series of carriers as baby gets older, choose a carrier that has versatility to be used from birth to two or three years and in various carrying positions. A fact of human nature is that if something is not convenient to use, we won't use it. Fathers especially shy away from carriers that have many buckles and straps. A versatile carrier is easily adjusted while being worn, so that baby is not unnecessarily disturbed.

We have noticed the best results with the sling-type carrier rather than the pack-type carrier. We prefer the sling because it meets all the criteria mentioned above, and more. The sling is more versatile to accommodate changing holding patterns with baby's changing size and development. In the early months, baby is cradled in parent's front, in close nursing distance, and mother can pull the sling up over the baby and breastfeed discreetly. The sling can allow for even an older baby's need to nurse at those inopportune times when you just can't get to a quiet, private place (such as standing in line at the grocery store).

As baby increases in weight and size and squirminess, he is shifted to the side, eventually allowing him to be carried on the hips and his weight evenly distributed between parent's shoulder and hip. For the fashion-conscious mother, the sling may even match or compliment her wardrobe. The new sling-type carriers are nurturing devices which make rediscovering this lost art easier for parents and make this a good time to be a baby.

At a recent international parenting conference, we interviewed two women from Zambia who were carrying their babies in slings that matched their native dress. We asked them why women in their culture wear their babies most of the time. One woman replied, "It makes life easier for the mother." The other volunteered, "It's good for the baby."

These women went on to relate the feeling of "completeness" and "value" that baby-wearing gives them. Women in their culture don't have the benefit of books and studies about mothering hormones. What they have are centuries of tradition that have taught them simply that something good and something valuable happens to women and their babies when the babies are worn.

CHAPTER NINE
Nighttime Parenting

"When will my baby sleep through the night?" is one of the most common concerns of new parents. Many baby books pronounce that babies should be sleeping through the night at three months. This unrealistic expectation leads parents to think that if their baby does not sleep well at night, either something is wrong with the baby or something is wrong with their parenting.

Nursing Down
Another common concern of tired parents is, "It takes me so long to get her to sleep." The reason babies don't settle easily is that the sequence of falling asleep is different for babies than adults. Adults are able to go from the state of being awake quickly into the state of deep sleep without passing through a long period of light sleep—we can "crash" easily. Babies, on the other hand, have to go through a much longer period of light sleep to get to the state of deep sleep. This pattern accounts for mothers often saying, "She has to be fast asleep before I can put her down." This biological

fact of sleep means that babies need to be *parented* to sleep, not just put to sleep.

The art of inducing sleep in your baby is achieved by rocking and gentling your baby through this period of light sleep into the deep sleep phase, when she is then able to be put down. Most mothers find inducing sleep easiest when they curl up and nestle close to their babies and nurse their babies through this period of light sleep into the deeper sleep phase, a sleep inducing style we call "nursing down."

Babies' Sleep Patterns

Babies' sleep patterns are different from adults'. When we fall asleep we progress through several stages of sleep, from a very light sleep to a very deep sleep. Most adults spend the greatest percentage of their total sleep time in a state of deep sleep, whereas tiny babies spend most of their time in a state of light sleep. If you watch your baby sleeping, you can easily identify which state of sleep she is in.

In a state of light sleep, which is the state of more active sleep from which baby is easily aroused, the baby appears asleep but she is squirming; her breathing movements are somewhat irregular. Sometimes her eyes are only partially closed and her eyeballs are moving. In fact, this state of light sleep is often called "REM" or rapid eye movement sleep. When a baby is in deep sleep, her body is much quieter and she seems totally zonked. Because her eyes are still during this period of sleep, this is often call "non-REM" sleep.

In the first few months of life, most babies sleep between fourteen to eighteen hours a day. A tiny baby's sleep patterns often resemble her feeding patterns—small frequent feedings and short frequent naps. In the first three months, most babies seldom sleep more than four hours at a stretch. As your baby gets older, she develops what is called sleep maturity, meaning that your baby enjoys (and, we hope, so do you) a larger percentage of total sleep time in deep sleep than in light sleep.

Another difference between sleep patterns of babies and adults is that babies have shorter sleep cycles. A sleep cycle is the total time spent going through both the "REM" and "non-REM" states of sleep. Adult sleep cycles last an average of ninety minutes. Infants' sleep cycles are shorter, lasting fifty to sixty minutes. During each sleep cycle, as the infant or adult ascends from a state of deep sleep to a state of light sleep, there is a vulnerable period for waking. Since babies have shorter sleep cycles, they may experience a vulnerable period for night waking every hour.

This Is God's Design?

At this point tired parents may be wondering why God designed babies to awaken so easily. There seem to be two reasons.

1. *Night waking may have survival benefits.* In the first few months, babies' needs are highest but their ability to communicate these needs is lowest. Suppose a baby slept most of the night. Some basic needs would go unfulfilled. Tiny babies have tiny tummies, and mother's milk is digested very rapidly. If a baby's stimulus of hunger could not easily arouse her, this would not be good for baby's survival. If a baby's nose were stuffed and she could not breathe or was cold and needed warmth, and her sleep state was so deep that she could not communicate her needs, her survival would be jeopardized.

2. *Secondly, night waking may have developmental benefits.* Sleep researchers theorize that the predominance of light sleep during the first year is important for the baby's brain. During the light sleep state, the higher centers of the brain keep operating, whereas during deep sleep these higher brain centers shut off and the baby functions on her lower brain centers. It is possible that during this stage of most rapid brain growth (baby's brain grows to seventy percent of its adult volume in the first year), the brain needs to continue functioning during sleep in order to develop. (On hearing this sleep theory, one worn-out mother exclaimed, "Well, in that case, my baby's going to be very, very smart.")

When your baby awakens during the night (for the third time), if you can have faith that God designed babies according to some nighttime plan that has both survival and developmental benefits, perhaps you can better accept your nighttime parenting.

Temperaments and Sleep Patterns

A tired new mother shared with us one day, "I must not be a good mother. My friend's baby sleeps through the night, but mine doesn't."

Mothers, please don't take responsibility for your own baby's individual sleep pattern—it may simply be a reflection of your baby's temperament.

In those old days of "calendar parenting," the effectiveness of a mother was measured by how soon her baby was sleeping through the night, eating three meals a day, weaned, and toilet trained. By this point, we hope you have heard our message that every baby has her own individual needs and calendar—you shouldn't try to fit her to someone else's notion of the "right" time for doing anything. The age at which babies settle varies tremendously from baby to baby.

One would think that more difficult and active babies should need more sleep (their parents do!); instead, high-need babies seem to carry their waking personalities into their sleep and have shorter periods of deep sleep, more night waking. Parents of the high-need baby may find this pretty unjust. "Why does my baby need more of everything but sleep?" one mom asked. But high-need babies are more sensitive babies both by day and by night.

Sharing Sleep

"When you lie down you will not be afraid; when you lie down, your sleep will be sweet" (Proverbs 3:24). Persistently tired babies and parents may find that verse a mockery. But we strongly feel that God would not have designed a baby with a sleep pattern too difficult for the parents to cope with.

Tired parents and tired babies simply do not enjoy their relationship in the way God has intended. We believe that parents do have the ability to help their baby organize her sleep patterns. Let's now discuss some tips on how to do this and how to widen your acceptance level to survive your baby's nighttime needs.

As a family, you must arrive at a sleeping arrangement that gets all three of you the most sleep and leaves all three of you feeling right. Some babies sleep better in their own bed in their own room; some babies sleep better in their own bed in their parents' room; and some babies sleep better in their parents' bed. Whichever works for your individual family is best for you.

"Sharing sleep" is a sleeping arrangement whereby you welcome your baby into your bed early in infancy, and your baby remains in your bed until she can comfortably sleep by herself. Many parents aren't sure about this. "Is it all right for our baby to sleep with us?" they ask. The answer is an unreserved, "Yes!" It is not only good to sleep with your baby, but we strongly feel that God intended the young of each species to sleep in close contact with the mother until such time when the baby can comfortably sleep independently.

This sleeping arrangement is sometimes called "the family bed." We prefer the term "sharing sleep," because this arrangement involves more than just sharing a place to sleep, it also means that parents and baby share sleep cycles and attitudes about sleep.

We have advocated the concept of sharing sleep in our own pediatric practice for the last twelve years, and we have practiced this arrangement in our own family. It is beautiful! It works! Perhaps this sleeping arrangement does not work for all families at all times, but in our experience it works for most families most of the time, provided it is done with the attitude that God has intended.

Sleeping close to or with the parents is a natural continuum from mother's womb to mother's breast to parents' bed, and weaning from all three of these places of security should only occur when mother and baby are ready.

The concept of sharing sleep is more an attitude than a decision about where your baby sleeps. It is an attitude of acceptance and mutual trust, whereby an infant learns to trust her parents as a continually available support resource during the night just as she trusts her parents during the day.

It is an attitude of trust for the parents, too. They are trustful of their inner feelings as to what feels right in their parenting of their child rather than accepting the cultural norms of the neighborhood or yielding to the dictates of peer pressure. It is often difficult for new parents to listen to and accept the cues of their infant and child as to what type of care-giving she needs. This is usually because of the many unfounded cultural taboos which have hampered intuitive child rearing and because of the unreasonable feeling that "I don't want my child to manipulate me," or "I don't want her to get into such a habit that she will never leave our bed."

Be open and accepting to whatever sleeping arrangements works for your family. If all three of you sleep better with your baby in your bed, and you all feel right about it, this arrangement is best for your family.

Advantages of Sharing Sleep

Sharing sleep helps babies organize their sleep patterns.
We have discussed that babies have a vulnerable period for waking up as they pass from the state of deep sleep into the state of light sleep. Since they have these sleep cycle changes every hour, baby is vulnerable to waking up during the night as often as once every hour. Sleeping with somebody, some familiar and predictable person, helps provide a consistent attachment to help baby get through this vulnerable period for night waking and resettle herself into the next stage of sleep before she is able to fully awaken.

Remember, in the first year, babies have not yet developed object permanency. When a thing (or person) is out of sight, it (or he or she) is out of mind.

Picture yourself when you awaken from sleep. We awaken in various states of confusion, but we can usually drift through this state of confusion into the next state of sleep without becoming awake because we know where we are. The security of knowing where we are is heightened by a familiar somebody right next to us.

Most babies do not have the ability to conceive of mother as existing somewhere else. When a baby awakens alone during this vulnerable period, this aloneness may keep her from peacefully resettling herself into the next stage of sleep. Instead, she awakens with a stressful cry.

With our babies, we found that waking up next to their most familiar attachment persons usually smoothed the transition from one state of sleep to the next and kept them from fully awakening, or at least helped them resettle into the next state of sleep without much separation anxiety.

We can tell when our baby is passing this vulnerable period of awakening because he often reaches out and touches one of us. When he reaches his anticipated target a smile appears, and an "I'm okay" expression radiates from his face, although his eyes remain closed and he does not fully awaken. This is one of the beautiful scenes of nighttime parenting that can only be realized by being open to your child at night.

Mothers sleep better.
This may come as a surprise to parents, but not only does baby sleep better when sharing sleep, but parents usually do also. The reason for this can be summed up in one word—harmony. We have previously discussed the importance of achieving harmony with your child during the day. Spending the night with your baby allows this harmony to continue, so that babies and mothers get their sleep cycles "in sync." Babies awaken their mothers during each other's light sleep cycles and sleep during each other's deep sleep cycles.

When this harmony is achieved, mothers are not awakened as often from their state of deep sleep. Being awakened from the state of deep sleep by a hungry and crying baby is what makes the concept of nighttime parenting unattractive and leads to exhausted mothers, fathers, and babies.

There are three situations which make the hormone *prolactin* (discussed in Chapter 6) increase in your body: sleeping, breastfeeding, and touching your baby. Sleeping with your baby allows all three of these conditions to occur throughout the night. When a baby shares sleep with the mother, she touches the mother and nurses from the mother, and this stimulates more prolactin to be released.

It is important to note that it is not nighttime that causes prolactin to go up, but the act of sleeping itself, whether by day or night. This is why we encourage mothers to take frequent naps and sleep with their baby during the day also—a custom we call "nap nursing."

Mothers who share sleep with their babies and have mastered this nighttime harmony often share with us that as time goes by they seem to need less sleep and feel more rested, despite the fact that their baby continues to awaken and nurse several times at night. Their acceptance and tolerance of nighttime mothering seems to widen. Is it possible that the increased prolactin could be responsible for the increase in tolerance for nighttime mothering?

Breastfeeding is easier.
When babies and mothers are in close nursing distance with each other, the nursing pair can often meet each other's needs without either person becoming fully awake.

MARTHA: *About thirty seconds before my baby awakened for his feeding, my sleep seemed to lighten and I would almost wake up. By being able to anticipate his feeding, I could usually start breastfeeding him just as he began to squirm and reach for the nipple. Getting to him immediately kept him from fully waking up, and then he drifted back into a deep sleep right after a brief nursing.*

What happened with this nursing pair is that baby probably nursed right through the vulnerable period for awakening and then reentered the state of deep sleep. If mother and baby had not been in close nursing distance with each other, the baby probably would have had to wake up crying to signify her need. By the time mother reached the baby in another room, both mother and baby would be wide awake and have trouble settling back to sleep.

Sharing sleep makes child spacing easier.
We are frequently asked to give our opinion on child spacing. Because there is such a wide variety of life-styles and family situations, child spacing is a very individual decision. It is

our feeling that God intended children to be spaced about three years apart. Our rationale for this is as follows: In cultures that practice natural mothering or the attachment style of parenting, yet use no means of artificial contraception, children are generally spaced at least three years apart.

Why doesn't this appear to work in western cultures? The reason is natural child spacing requires playing the game by the rules, and the number one rule is unrestricted breastfeeding. The hormone stimulated by breastfeeding naturally suppress the hormones which promote ovulation. Unrestricted breastfeeding implies sharing sleep with the baby, because it is true that babies that share sleep with the mother do feed more frequently at night. In the western world, we are programmed toward day time feeding and night sleeping, although babies may not have been designed that way. The reason that breastfeeding does not work as a natural contraceptive in our culture is not a fault of the design or the Designer, but is due to the fact that we have not followed the design. In our experience, natural family planning seldom works unless mothers and babies share sleep.

If you and your baby are enjoying the shared sleep arrangement, be prepared for negative reactions. Someone is bound to warn you, "You'll be sorry. You'll never be able to get her out of your bed." We'll discuss ways to respond to such comments in Chapter 12, "Handling Criticism."

Babies who enjoy sleeping with their parents do not want to willingly give up this arrangement. Once you have achieved harmony, why settle for disharmony? But babies who have shared sleep with their parents early on eventually turn out to be more independent children and have fewer sleep disturbances as older children. This is because they develop a *healthy sleep attitude*; they learn to regard sleep as a pleasant time, a time of closeness, whereas children who sleep alone (especially if they don't want to sleep alone) often grow up regarding sleep as a fearful time, a time of separation.

There is no set age when at which a baby or child will stop sleeping with her parents; a gradual weaning process will be required, just as with breastfeeding. The most practical sharing sleep arrangement seems to be where baby sleeps between mother and a guard-rail rather than between mom and dad.

An alternative option, if having your baby in bed with you is not attractive (bed too small, etc.) is the side car arrangement, in which baby sleeps in a crib adjacent to your bed with the nearest side rail of the crib removed. Place the two mattresses tightly together at the same height. This arrangement still gets mother and baby in close nursing distance with each other but allows baby and parents their separate space.

The sharing sleep style of nighttime parenting is especially valuable in families with busy lifestyles who are away from their baby a lot during the day. This style of parenting allows you to give "I care" messages to your child all during the night, without even saying a word.

There are probably many beneficial effects of sharing sleep that are in the divine design which we do not yet understand. Some researchers have even suggested that mothers' and babies' sleep and dream cycles and brain wave patterns are in unison when they sleep and nurse together. Science is only just beginning to understand what God has designed and what intuitive mothers have known all along: something good happens when babies and mothers sleep in touch with each other.

CHAPTER TEN

Your Baby's Mind

"I wonder what my baby is thinking." Because the infant cannot tell us what he is thinking, we must deduce what the infant thinks by the way he acts. In this section we will discuss cognitive development—what the infant thinks and how he "reasons." We will attempt to simplify the latest research in cognitive development based upon a survey of the most reliable studies as well as our own observations.

One of the newest concepts of cognitive development (one not appreciated by early researchers) is the profound effect that sensitive and responsible care givers can have on the intellectual development of the infant.

For example: Baby cries and is picked up and nursed. The lips are very rich in nerve endings, and the intense sucking of the newborn baby stimulates these nerve fibers to send impulses to the brain. These impulses need to be processed and connected to the other nerves within the brain.

For example: During nursing the infant sees mother's face. The nerves of the infant's eyes transmit the image of the face to the area of the brain that processes visual information, and the infant stores the image of this face. Repeatedly seeing a familiar face stimulates the infant to want to react, thus stimulating some connections between the nerves within the visual centers of the brain and the nerves controlling the muscles.

For example: Touch is considered by brain researchers to be a powerful enhancer of brain development because of the rich supply of nerves within the skin. This is scientifically discussed in a classic book, *Touching*, by Dr. Ashley Montague. He theorizes that the human brain is purposely underdeveloped at birth so that the head is not too large to pass through the birth canal. He also feels that the human infant needs a continued womb-like environment for an additional nine months in order to enhance brain development.

Responsiveness to baby's cries . . . nursing . . . high touch . . . if you think this is beginning to sound like another argument for attachment parenting, you're absolutely right. Any discussion of cognitive development of the infant must take into account the response of the care giving environment to the signals of the infant. In reality, we should be discussing the *cognitive development of the family unit*.

Care Givers and Cognitive Development

Both parent and infant develop the responses of each other. Baby's initial stimulus is reflexive (a need generates crying), mother's is cognitive (should I pick up and nurse?). As the pair practices this cue-response behavior, the baby's actions become more cognitive (if I cry I get picked up and nursed) and the mother's responses become more intuitive, ultimately leading to a predictable and harmonious pattern of behavior of the pair.

Patterns of behavior

With repetition of patterns of response such as "distress followed by comfort," the infant develops a pattern of behavior which infant developmentalists refer to as a schema. Although the initial behavior of the infant is reflexive or non-cognitive, the repeated response of the care giver to the reflex signal gradually enables the infant to learn a cognitive behavior.

The sequence is as follows: hunger stimulates a reflex signal—cry; response—pick up and nurse; result—hunger satisfied. Repetition of this sequence equals a pattern of behavior or a schema.

The infant seems to store this pattern of behavior. Eventually, when picked up he anticipates that picking up will be followed by nursing. He begins to orient toward the breast. Thus the infant clicks into a pre-set pattern of behavior. When picked up he anticipates that nursing will follow and learns to orient toward mother's breast in anticipation of a pleasurable action.

If we compare the development of an infant's brain to a record in which grooves are cut following a stimulus, each time a stimulus occurs the infant clicks into a pre-set groove (pattern of behavior) and responds accordingly. Various other grooves then are mapped throughout the brain which cause the infant to click into this pre-set groove, such as orienting toward the breast in response to the stimulus of hunger.

A predictably responsive environment in which the infant anticipates and trusts that a response will soon follow causes these grooves to develop better. Unpredictable responses, on the other hand, confuse the infant and may cause disorganized or shallower grooves to be formed in the infant's developing brain.

Competence
Competence means abilities. An infant develops increasing motor competence when he improves his abilities to get from one place to another, first by crawling and then later by walking. We say that this infant has increased his loco-motor competence. Most infant competencies imply not only what the infant is able to do by himself, but also his ability to enlist the help of care givers. For example, the development of social competence, the ability to enlist the help of others, depends a great deal on how responsive the care givers are to the infant's cues for assistance. It may, therefore, be more correct to discuss the competencies of the parent-infant pair, rather than the infant alone.

If a highly competent infant is paired with a less sensitively responsive mother, this infant is less likely to develop his social competence to his fullest potential, nor is the mother likely to develop hers. If a less competent infant is paired with a highly responsive mother, the infant is likely to improve his competencies. If a highly competent infant is paired with a highly responsive mother, both members of the pair are likely to develop their social competence to their fullest potential. The influence of responsive parents is well illustrated by the following experiments.

Researchers compared the sensitivity of mothers' responsiveness to their infants' crying to the infants' later development of communication skills. They found that the infants of highly sensitive mothers (those who gave a prompt nurturant response to their infants' crying) developed better communication skills toward the end of the first year, i.e., they had developed better social competence. Infant developmentalists feel that the development of social competence may have a carryover effect in assisting the infant to become more competent in all developmental skills by fostering an overall "sense of competence."

Intelligence Quotient
The following parenting traits, listed in order of importance, are shown to exert a positive effect on infant I.Q.

1. Maternal sensitivity and responsiveness to infant signals.

2. High maternal verbal and physical contact, a harmonious mother-infant attachment, reinforcement of the infant's verbal cues, and frequency of interchange during play.

3. Acceptance of and going with the flow of infant's temperament.

4. Floor freedom—permitting baby freedom of movement to explore the world and providing a stimulating environment of toys and play activities which encourage decision making and problem solving.

Those factors which negatively influenced infant I.Q. were low maternal verbal and physical contact, high restrictiveness of exploration, and frequent punishment. It is interesting that parental education was not significantly correlated with infant I.Q. in the infants studied at eight and eleven months.

In essence, parents contribute greatly to early learning by creating the conditions which allow learning to occur. Infants learn best in the behavioral state of quiet alertness. Attachment parenting fosters quiet alertness and this is how parents create the conditions to help their baby learn.

Motor Abilities

The infant's motor abilities develop from head to toe, so the earliest motor connections are to the face. Eventually, the stimulus of the parent's face causes the visual area of the brain to send out a message to the motor area which controls the infant's facial muscles. The result is a smile. If the environmental stimuli affecting neurological development are repeated, connections are made with other motor areas so eventually baby can reach out and touch his mother's or father's face with his hands and even later with his feet. The moral of this neurological story is that the more the infant has organized interaction with his environment, the more brain connections he is able to develop.

God designed the infant brain to grow at a rate which fits in beautifully with the infant's individual rate of motor development. The function of the infant's brain occurs on a level which is best suited for the infant to survive and thrive in the environment at a certain age. If one part of the brain were more mature than the other, the infant would not fit well into his environment. As we already mentioned, the infant brain develops from head to toe, in that the nerves controlling the structures of the face and arms develop before those of the feet.

Suppose it were not this way, and a newborn came into the world being able to walk just as well as he is able to suck. (Other species, such as range animals, are born being able to walk right after birth, because their legs are their

main survival system.) Attachment to the mother is the
survival system for the human infant, so that the development of motor capabilities occurs much later in the human
species.

The Amazing Brain
Between birth and one year the brain doubles in size, reaching around sixty percent of its adult volume. All the cells in
the human brain are generated before birth; no new cells
are added during extra-uterine life but some may be taken
away. As the brain grows, branches of these nerve cells—
called neurons—proliferate like miles of tangled electrical
wires. The infant is born with much of this wiring uncon-
nected. No new neurons grow after birth, but plenty of
new connections, or synapses, are made. During the first
year, these neurons grow larger, learn to work better, and
connect up with each other to make circuits which enable
baby to think and do more things.

Each neuron is composed of three parts: a set of branch-
ing nerves called *dendrites*, the cell body, and another set of
nerves called an *axon*. The dendrites receive a message and
pass this message into the cell body. The cell body processes and stores the message and sends out its own message
to the axon. The tips of the axons branch out like feelers
attempting to make connections with other nerves.

After birth, two important improvements are made in
this system. Each neuron acquires a coating called *myelin*
which helps the messages move faster and, as it were,
insulates the nerves, preventing short circuits. Secondly,
the number of synapses between nerves increases due to
the development of a nerve growth factor which stimulates
neurons to make connections.

Although the number of neurons is fixed at birth, the
number of connections can indeed change. If nerve cells
don't make connections they die; the more connections
they make, the better the brain develops. Brain researchers
suggest that *it is these connections that we can influence* in a
child, thus making him "smarter." Attachment parenting
helps the baby's developing brain *make the right connections.*

Many studies now show that the most powerful enhancers of brain development are the quality of the parent-infant attachment and the response of the care giving environment to the cues of the infant. We contend that attachment parenting actually promotes brain development by feeding the brain with the right kind of stimulation at a time in a child's life when the brain needs the most nourishment.

Stages of Cognitive Development

Expressed simply, the infant's first year of cognitive development is divided into four stages: birth to one month, one to four months, four to eight months, and eight to twelve months. These stages are very general, since there is a wide variability in cognitive development from infant to infant.

Birth to one month: the fitting-in stage
During this stage the newborn learns to fit into the care giving environment. In order to fit, the newborn comes programmed with qualities called attachment promoting behaviors—automatic behaviors which are programmed into the baby to get the parent-infant care system rolling. Throughout development the infant refines these attachment promoting behaviors to strengthen and cement the bond to his parents.

The most noticeable of these attachment promoting behaviors is the infant's cries. The newborn's cries are undifferentiated. The cry may mean hunger, cold, or distress. A newborn seldom shows different cries for different needs, nor does the parent perceive different signals for different needs. These early newborn cries are largely automatic reflexes. He does not think "I'm hungry, now I must cry to get fed." Part of cognitive development is to refine these reflexive behaviors such as crying into cognitive behaviors in which the infant "thinks" before he acts.

The more sensitive and responsive the care giver is to the cues of infant, the better these early reflex behaviors translate into thought-out behaviors. One of the first things the infant "learns" is anticipation. He learns that his signals result in a response. For example, "I cry, I get picked up and nursed." With continued repetition of the cue-response pattern, the infant learns to match his expectancies to his responses and develops a model of what his care giving world should be.

One to four months

Patterns of behavior, or schemas, become the first building blocks for cognitive development. The next advance is refining these patterns of behavior to improve their outcome. For example, the infant clicks into a pattern of behavior by sucking. By repeated variations on the pattern of sucking, he learns to suck in a way to get milk more efficiently. The newborn routinely initiates a breastfeeding session with continuous sucking for thirty-sixty seconds before the milk ejection reflex occurs, and then he starts to suck-swallow as the flow of milk begins.

In studying our sixth child, Matthew, we noticed that he learned to simply latch on, give several sucks, and then wait for the anticipated milk ejection reflex, at which time he began to suck-swallow. As the baby practices his sucking skills and his central nervous system matures, the infant makes adjustments in these patterns of behavior. In the newborn period, most of a baby's behavior is directed toward the goals of comfort and satisfaction. In this stage the patterns of behavior come more under the infant's control.

The infant at this stage learns contingency actions, i.e., a certain reaction from his environment is contingent upon the baby initiating the action. For example: "I hit the mobile, the mobile moves." The baby learns cause and effect. He can cause the mobile to move. The combination of contingency actions learned during this stage and the early foundation of trust and organization developed during the previous stage results in a major developmental cognitive milestone: the development of competence. The infant learns that persons and objects in his environment are responsive to him. Competence and trust are the roots of the infant's self esteem.

134

During the stage of one to four months, the infant's rapidly developing central nervous system functions—mainly visual acuity, head control, and arm and hand movements—all complement his cognitive development. New patterns of behavior are developed and more adjustments are made to refine these patterns.

For example, baby can now see mother clearly a few feet away. This visual skill, coupled with better head control, allows baby to develop the pattern of behavior of gazing at mother and studying her facial gestures. He develops an image of familiarity: No one looks like, smiles, or sounds like her. Baby's developing smiles and cues help to hold the attention of the care giver longer and further reinforce other developmental skills. Because the infant enjoys these new social overtures from the mother, he responds by increasing his social gestures. This is mutual feedback and reinforcement. During this interaction, baby locks into the schema of mother as a social person in addition to the previous schema of mother as a comforter.

During face to face interaction, if mother moves slowly to one side of the baby, baby makes adjustments in his pattern of behavior to keep a fix on mother. He learns that by moving his eyes and head he can sustain this interaction. However, if mother moves beyond seeing distance or into another room, baby loses her because he does not yet have the mental ability to reproduce the image of mother—out of sight is still out of mind. Baby will either fuss because the schema or "groove" that he was in is gone, or he will switch into another groove such as self comforting by thumb sucking.

Enter the father. A different groove is set down. Father looks different, smells different, sounds different. He gives and responds to social cues differently. A different pattern of behavior is set up.

BILL: *During Matthew's early months, our daily walks had a definite pattern. I would pick Matthew up, nestle him, then begin singing and walking. After a few months of this, as soon as I picked Matthew up, the baby immediately nestled into the groove, anticipating that a song and walk were soon to follow.*

135

Early on in this stage, baby's pattern of behavior centers around his own body or social reactions to the care giver's body. Toward the end of this stage the ability to use his hands as tools facilitates a giant leap in cognitive development—decision making that can be acted out. By developing the hand skills to reach out and manipulate his environment, baby can now "decide" how to use them. Motor skills of reaching and grabbing naturally imply making decisions as to when and how to reach and what to do with the toy once he has grabbed it. Decision making results in another cognitive refinement—accommodation. Baby makes in-flight corrections during his reaching out for the toy, as if having to use his mind more to make his hands work better.

During this stage of development the infant is not just a passive player in the game of parent-infant development, as was previously thought. The infant takes a very active part in engaging and holding the attention of his care givers. The more sensitively these care givers respond, the more the infant is stimulated to refine those cues which engage in holding the care giver's attention. It seems much of an infant's intellectual development is truly bound up in this early attachment relationship.

Four to eight months—the sensory-motor stage
In the previous stage, the infant-development patterns of behavior were primarily oriented toward himself—what gave him pleasure and comfort. This next stage is called the sensory-motor period because the infant learns about the world primarily through the use of his senses and the motor activities of his body. The infant expands his interests to include persons and toys outside of himself. The developing infant becomes increasingly capable of clicking in to more than one groove at a time.

The two developmental skills that prompt a rapid surge in cognitive development are the development of hand skills and locomotion. These skills enable the infant to nurture his developing sense of intentionality, leading to the most potent stimuli for cognitive development: decision making leading to problem solving. Hand skills allow a baby to pick up blocks of varying size, to pick up more than one block, to "figure out" how one block may fit on top of another, to decide the many different activities he can do with a block (banging, stacking, dropping) and to solve the problem of how to pick up a third block if he has one in each hand already. The primary pattern of behavior (picking up the block), or the big groove, branches out into many little grooves or associated patterns of behavior— the many fun activities he can do with the blocks once he has grabbed them. The basic decision-making process of "which one to pick up and what to do with it" is an exciting step forward in cognitive development.

Locomotion (crawling) stimulates cognitive development to take a giant leap forward. Locomotion fosters more problem solving and decision making. For example, baby sees a block across the room. He "knows" that he has the locomotor competency to reach the block. He clicks into the locomotor groove, as it were, and crawls toward the block. Upon reaching the block he clicks into another pre-set groove or pattern of behavior, hand skills, and then picks up and manipulates the block.

During this stage the brain centers for feeling and expressions of emotion also develop. This surge in central nervous system development, coupled with the baby's increasing realization that there are certain goals that he cannot attain with his current physical abilities (e.g., dropping the toy from the high chair, losing it, not being able to find it) inevitably leads to the feelings of frustrations and expressions of these feelings—the emergence of temperamental behavior. Just as these frustrations lead to undesirable behavior, the increasing holding power that the baby shows to engage his care givers in increasingly exciting play activities also results in baby's showing more positive temperamental features of delight, such as hilarious laughing.

Toward the end of this stage, the locomotor abilities allow baby to separate from the mother, but they also bring on frustration of not being able to handle separation from the mother. This is called *separation anxiety*. As baby does not yet possess the cognitive ability of object permanence, out of sight is still out of mind. By maintaining voice contact with the baby, the mother, who can be heard but not seen, stimulates baby to develop a mental image of her. This is another example of how attachment promotes cognitive development.

The separation anxiety that is so characteristic of this stage is the reason why one of the most important concepts of weaning is that *the infant should separate from the mother and not the mother from the infant.* Given the normal attachment model, the infant will not separate from the mother completely until he has the cognitive abilities to develop a mental image of the mother and, as it were, take the mother with him. It is beautiful to see how God designed both the locomotor and mental capabilities to develop together and to be mutually dependent on each other as long as the care giving environment creates the conditions which allow them to complement but not frustrate each other.

Eight to twelve months—the development of memory
During this stage, the infant greatly increases his ability to store and retrieve information. One of the most important aspects of cognitive development, person and object permanence, develops at this stage. Previously the out-of-sight-out-of-mind concept prevailed. When a toy was hidden under a cloth, the infant turned away and quickly lost interest, not making a consistent effort to pursue the toy. In this stage, missing toys and missing persons seem to take on a permanence because of the mental image of the toys and persons stored up in the infant's mind.

Even at this stage, memory is still rudimentary and often needs some trigger to set the memory in process. For example, mother is in another room and baby fusses. When mother hears the baby fussing and makes voice contact with the baby—"Mama's coming"—baby will often momentarily stop fussing, as if mother's voice triggered off a mental image of her. While reflecting on the mental image of mother, baby seems momentarily satisfied that the mother is present.

The ability to retain mental images of a familiar care giver is thought to provide a secure base, so that the infant can more easily and less anxiously progress from the familiar to the unfamiliar. The infant is now able to focus on a mental image of one pattern of behavior (e.g., mother comforting) while simultaneously engaging in another pattern of behavior (exploring a new area of the house). These new mental capabilities allow the infant to, in effect, take mother with him as he crawls further away from her to explore and learn from his environment. This is a classic example of how cognitive development fosters motor development, which in turn fosters more cognitive development.

Another interesting feature of the secure base hypothesis is what we call the "deep groove theory." Suppose the strength of mother-infant attachment is represented by a deeper groove in baby's mental record. Early theorists in infant behavior popularized the spoiling theory, which held that if the infant was too strongly attached to the mother he would never get out of this groove to become independent and explore his world.

Research has shown the opposite to be true. The most securely attached infants, the ones with the "deepest grooves," actually show less anxious separation from the mother while exploring toys in the same room with the mother. These infants periodically checked in with mother (returning to the groove) for a sort of emotional refueling, seeking mother's reassuring message. The mother seems to add energy to the infant's exploration. Since the infant does not need to waste energy worrying about home base, he uses that energy to further explore, and therefore separates less anxiously. An infant with a shallower attachment groove may not avail himself of this energy conservation system.

Our deep groove theory may also explain why infants will not accept alternative need satisfiers. For example, some breastfed infants refuse to take a bottle. This is because a bottle does not fit into their anticipated pattern of behavior.

When going from oneness to separateness, the securely attached baby establishes a balance between his desire to explore and encounter new situations and his continued need for the safety and contentment provided by mother. During each stage of development, a baby strives for an equilibrium between oneness and separateness. This balance is disturbed in one of two ways: Baby encounters a novel toy or a stranger, which disturbs baby beyond his coping level. Another possibility is that the mother leaves, thus reducing the baby's sense of security and the amount of novelty he can seek out. The result is that the baby feels compelled to reestablish his original equilibrium by calling out to his mother or retreating from the strange situation.

If during a strange place situation the infant moves closer to the mother or the mother moves closer to the infant, a sort of "go ahead" message emanates from the mother, providing the infant with the confidence to explore and handle the strange situation. A new and higher balance is established, so that the next time a similar situation is encountered the infant has confidence to handle it by himself without the mother.

Exploratory relationships in which the mother is consistently and emotionally available promote independence, confidence, and trust, leading to the ultimate in cognitive development of oneness and separateness—the capacity to be alone.

Early researchers in attachment theory suggested that a child with no confidence does not trust that his attachment figures will be accessible to him when he needs them. He adopts a clinging strategy to insure that they will be available. He is uncertain of the mother's availability and thus is always preoccupied with it. This preoccupation hinders separation and exploration, and therefore baby's learning.

The Payoff

We believe that the most important effect of a parenting style on cognitive development is that the infant who is the product of a sensitive and nurturing environment develops in his mind the model of the world as a nurturing place to be. In adult jargon we call this a "mindset." Infants of the attachment style of parenting develop a *nurturing mindset.*

They learn to relate to people more than things. They become high-touch children in a high-tech world.

The high-touch infant has cut such deep grooves in his memory record that he learns the quality of intimacy. The infant learns to give and receive love. He becomes capable of strong attachments, using his mindset of parent-infant attachment as the standard to measure all future attachments—and ultimately learning how to develop an attachment with God. Given the style of parenting according to God's design, as the child goes from oneness to separateness from his parents, he is then prepared to go from separateness to oneness with God.

CHAPTER ELEVEN

Discipline Begins at Birth

We enjoy giving parenting seminars to couples expecting their first baby and to parents of young babies. Most of our seminars are about helping parents get the right start with their newborn by practicing attachment parenting. One evening we decided to change the title of our seminar to "How to Discipline Your Child"—but we changed only the title, not the content. The course began with a discussion of the importance of preparing for your newborn, bonding with your baby, nursing your baby, responding promptly to your baby's cries, wearing your baby—the whole style of attachment parenting.

About halfway through the class, an impatient father politely interrupted: "Can we discuss discipline so I can keep my child from being unruly?" We assured this dad that we had been talking about discipline all along. Every interaction you have with your child helps to discipline that child.

Early in our parenting career and in the practice of pediatrics, we considered discipline as primarily what a parent does *to* a child in the second year of life, when the conflict of wills begin. We soon realized that this is only a part of the picture.

Laying a foundation of discipline begins as soon as your child is born. What you want to do is to create an attitude within your child and an atmosphere within your home that assumes that punishment won't often be necessary, and when it is necessary it will be administered appropriately. There are two aspects to laying this foundation: knowing your child and helping your child feel right.

Knowing Your Child

Christian parents can always quote verses like Colossians 3:20: "Children, obey your parents in everything, for this pleases the Lord." But the Hebrew word for obey means to "hear intelligently." We infer from this that in order for a child to obey, or hear intelligently, the parent must speak the language of discipline that the child understands. A close attachment between parent and child helps the parent connect to the child in such a way that the parent feels he is getting through to the child and the child under-stands the parent. Although it is clear that God gives parents a mandate to take charge of their children, in order to carry out this mandate, we must first *know* our children.

"I obey . . . for all my ways are known to you" says the psalmist (Psalm 119:168). If a child feels that her parents know her, she is more likely to obey them, because she trusts that they know what is best for her. One of the complaints we hear from older children about the way their parents discipline is, "My parents just don't understand me." It is vitally important that a child feels that her position is correctly understood, even though you may not necessarily agree with it. This begins in the first year, when a tiny baby feels understood because she is growing up in an environment that is responsive to her cues.

We also want our children to know us, because there is a connection between knowledge and trust—just as the more we know God the more we trust in Him. Psalm 9:10 says, "Those who know your name will trust in you." You don't trust somebody you don't know.

On occasion in our home, when a child is caught at a misdeed, he or she exclaims in amazement, "Mom, how did you know?" Mom knew because she was used to getting into that child's mind from birth on, as each developed an inner knowledge and trust of the other.

Helping Your Child Feel Right

Scripture shows clearly that every human being is born with a bent toward wrongdoing:

> "Folly is bound up in the heart of a child." (Proverbs 22:15)

> "Surely I have been a sinner from birth, sinful from the time my mother conceived me." (Psalm 51:5)

But in our opinion, if a child's nature is completely filled early on with the things which enhance her good nature, this good nature will prevail over the bad nature later. This is what attachment parenting does. An attachment-parented child learns and feels trust. Her needs have been consistently and responsively filled. Distress is always followed by comfort. She develops an inner sense of confidence and competence. In essence, she feels right.

The baby who is used to feeling right doesn't like feeling wrong. The parents have created an environment in which the baby does not have to fret. She learns what behavior evokes a pleasing response and is therefore programmed toward repeating this desirable behavior. She is motivated to be good. A child who *feels* right is more likely to *act* right.

This feeling of rightness as a basis for discipline is well illustrated in the Psalms.

> "O Lord, do not rebuke me in your anger or discipline me in your wrath." (Psalm 6:1)

> "You have made my lot secure." (Psalm 16:5)

> "I desire to do your will, O my God." (Psalm 40:8)

> "The law of God is in his heart." (Psalm 37:31)

Respect for Authority

Throughout Scripture we read of the association between love, knowledge, and trust forming the basis of our relationship with God and the way He disciplines those He loves. Throughout these verses there is also a clear picture that God is truly in charge. He is an authority.

From a biblical standpoint, much of discipline is bringing a child into submission to the will of someone in authority. A tiny baby has the language of needs, and the infant's first view of "authority" is someone who fills her needs. To a baby, an authority figure equals a need filler. A parent forms the first role as authority figure within minutes after birth. Your baby cries, and you comfort her. As this need-filling nurturing sequence is repeated hundreds of times during the early months, the more your baby trusts that distress will be followed by comfort—and the more you trust in your methods of comforting. Because your baby trusts your response, and you trust your response, you are learning to be a good disciplinarian—an effective authority figure.

God, our role model of the perfect father, is portrayed in Scripture as a source of strength, a strict disciplinarian, a limit setter, and, perhaps more importantly, a nurturer. "As a mother comforts her child, so I will comfort you" (Isaiah 66:13). In Numbers 11:12 (the Amplified Bible), Moses is referred to as a "nursing father" in his role to the Israelites.

The more you comfort your baby, the more confidence you have in your ability to read your baby. Your baby learns to regard you as a source of comfort and trust you as a nurturer. Having built the foundation of nurturing and trust, your later role as disciplinarian and authority figure becomes much more effective.

The Good Disciplinarian

One day I was watching a mother care for her baby. She nursed her baby on cue, comforted him when upset, played with him when she read his playful moods, and generally nurtured her baby very sensitively. Mother and baby seemed to be in harmony.

I couldn't resist saying to her, "You're a good disciplinarian."

She was understandably puzzled by my statement, because like most parents she was accustomed to thinking of discipline as a science of methods or techniques. I went on to explain to her just what I meant.

In our observation of patients over a period of ten years, one of our questions was, "What makes a well-disciplined child?"

The parents whose children seemed easiest to discipline, inherently less angry, and more respectful toward their parents were those who had practiced attachment parenting. These parents had developed the following qualities that made them more effective disciplinarians:

1. They are more observant of their infants' actions.
2. They respond intuitively to their infants' cues.
3. They are more confident in the appropriateness of their responses.
4. The fathers are more involved and nurturing.
5. They are sensitive to the feelings and circumstances that promote a particular behavior.
6. They know how to convey expected behavior to their children.
7. They have more realistic expectations of childhood behavior.
8. They have a wider acceptance of what is normal for their children's behavior and are less provoked to anger.
9. They learn the true meaning of giving of themselves.
10. They seek prayer and counsel when the going gets tough.

While it is true that there are many good books on discipline techniques and methods, these just do not work as well unless used with a foundation of knowing your child and helping your child feel right. Methods are effective when built on a foundation of mutual trust and mutual knowing that flows from the attachment style of parenting.

Discipline should not be a list of methods of external forces suggested by some third-party adviser. Only you can know the heart of your child and only you have the ability to discern what your baby's needs and feelings are. Relying on someone else's general method to discipline your individual child can doom a parent to disappointment. We believe God designed discipline to flow naturally from the inner harmony between a parent and child who really know one another.

Attachment parenting lays a foundation for discipline by the tremendous confidence it builds in parents who are struggling to take charge of the child they love. How rewarding it is to truly feel that you know your child so intimately that your discipline automatically flows from part of yourself. Without the basis of trust and knowledge, discipline can become strained and uncomfortable.

Pray daily that God will help you know your child and help him feel right, and that you will discipline your child in the same way God disciplines His children—with instruction and correction based on intimacy and respect.

Consequences of Restrained Parenting

When parents use a more restrained approach with their infants, cries are not consistently or appropriately responded to and distress is not consistently met with comfort. Parents and baby have a more shallow attachment. This baby operates from a basis of mistrust instead of trust, anxiety rather than rightness. In our experience, the probable result of this style of parenting is an angry baby—a baby difficult to discipline. Angry babies breed parents who are also prone to anger when they discipline.

Usually because of fear of "spoiling the child" or "being manipulated," these parents do not interact with their baby as much and thereby violate the two foundations of effective discipline. The more restrained style of parenting not only produces a baby who does not feel right; it also causes parents not to know their baby as well.

Consequently, having diluted their intuitive responses to their baby, discipline becomes a series of trial and error methods gleaned from a variety of third-party disciplinarians who do not know their child and who have no biological intuitive attachment to their child. Because their child "will not obey," the parents become frustrated with the child and with parenting in general. A distance develops between parents and child because of the absence of mutual sensitivity that should have developed during the first year. These parents are at risk for using corporal punishment as their prime mode of discipline.

To Spank or Not to Spank

Spanking is the most controversial of all methods of discipline, especially among Christian parents. We feel that the prevalence of spanking among Christian parents is due to the importance that they place on following God's mandate to discipline our children. Unfortunately, this is coupled with confusion over what Scripture says about corporal punishment.

In our opinion, nowhere in the Bible does it say you must spank your child to be a good Christian parent. There are no references to spanking in the New Testament; on the contrary, Christ taught sensitivity, gentleness, and love. This teaching was carried over by the Apostle Paul: "Shall I come to you with a whip, or in love and with a gentle spirit?" (I Corinthians 4:21).

The "rod verses" in the Old Testament, on which well-meaning Christian authors and teachers have based their discipline (Proverbs 13:24, 22:15, 23:13, and 29:15), are open to confusing interpretation. The "rod" could be interpreted as a tool for guiding or for beating the child. We believe the former is the intended meaning.

Be discerning in what you read on the subject of spanking. In teaching any subject, especially a sensitive one like this, the author's dictum should be based upon three sources: a vast personal experience with the issue, personal research and collaboration with trusted colleagues, and a careful interpretation of scriptural teachings. Parents are too vulnerable and children too valuable for authoritative teaching to be based upon anything but these sources.

Unfortunately, many Christian writers who have distinguished themselves in other avenues of teaching have gotten beyond their own field of expertise when teaching about discipline. Most teachings are based upon personal opinion, tempered somewhat by minimal personal experience with children and questionable interpretation of Scripture.

The basis of our opinions concerning discipline and spanking are based upon twenty years in pediatric practice and interaction with approximately 10,000 families, rearing our own seven children, discussion with authorities experienced and knowledgeable in the field of child development, and a study of Scripture. From these sources we have concluded that spanking is at the bottom of the list of methods for effective discipline.

Quite honestly, in the majority of families and over the long haul, spanking doesn't work. Spanking is often done to get the child to obey quickly, forgetting that true and lasting obedience is a long and gradual process which begins with the principles of attachment parenting we have discussed throughout this book.

We have collected feedback from hundreds of patients in our practice, those who have used spanking as a major mode of discipline and those who have not. In the overwhelming majority of families, when the child's behavior is spank controlled, a distance rather than a closeness develops between parent and child.

As we study the children with discipline problems in our practice, one feature stands out: these children usually operate from the basis of anger rather than trust. An angry child is the most difficult to discipline.

We have noticed that parents who practice the attachment style of parenting spank less (or not at all) because (1) they realize that lasting obedience doesn't come from the quick fix of spanking, (2) they are so sensitive and know their children so well that they find creative alternatives, and (3) the basis of mutual trust and sensitivity allows their children to be less angry and have more of a desire to please.

In developing your own approach to discipline, find support and role models in like-minded friends. Many young people we know, discouraged by the lack of peer support for their beliefs, have formed their own Bible study and parent support group for sharing experiences and ideas about how the attachment style of parenting works for them.

Beware of the fear that attachment parenting creates a manipulative and dependent child. Throughout this book we have stressed that the opposite is true. Our own experience, and that of other researchers, has shown that children disciplined according to these attachment principles achieve a healthy independence and the parents become healthy authority figures for their children.

One of our goals in writing this book is to help parents better enjoy their children. The attachment style of parenting gives you the basic tools from which you can branch off into a style of discipline that works for the individual temperament of your child and the life-style of your family.

CHAPTER TWELVE

Handling Criticism

One of the built-in hazards of attachment style parenting (or of any style parenting, for that matter) is the inevitable criticism that you will receive from friends and relatives. Your response is crucial, because criticism poorly handled can undermine your confidence as a parent and even keep you from your ultimate goals.

Several years ago we became aware of a survey done by Janet Jendron, a La Leche League leader from South Carolina, who now serves on the board of directors for La Leche League, International. The results of this survey are presented here in abbreviated form, because we feel that they can be a valuable tool in helping young couples, especially young mothers, learn how to handle criticism of their mothering.

Analyzing Your Response
From whom does criticism bother you the most?
More women find criticism from their husbands most troublesome, because a husband is closely involved with the children and emotionally involved with the mother. At

the same time, however, most women said that they rarely received criticism from their husbands.

A very tender spot is criticism from one's own mother. Most of us still have a deep innate desire to please our parents, especially our mothers and especially on this particular issue. There are many deep-rooted, intangible feelings involved in mother-daughter interaction about raising children.

Some people are most bothered by criticism from people who don't have children, for obvious reasons. Although it's true these people don't have the "right" to criticize, it never helps to have a defiant attitude toward their comments.

What areas of criticism bother you most?
The area named by most people with the most intensity was mother-baby togetherness. Many reasons were given, but most of them centered around the fact that people who don't understand mother-child togetherness are usually not thinking from the child's point of view. Criticism in this area is threatening because it implies a lack of trust in our ability to know our own children.

Another area that is bothersome is criticism from people who take a superior attitude about their regulated, controlled mothering, implying that we are out of control.

We are most likely to overreact when we are questioned about our most unsure areas. It's always worth considering the possibility that some criticism might have some truth to it.

In what situations are you most bothered by criticism?
Sometimes when we are in a group with our children, criticism is more threatening because it takes so much more energy to use creative methods of discipline (and we are distracted ourselves by trying to talk to the adults in the group). Discipline situations have a way of coming up every day, whereas other topics, such as sharing sleep or weaning, aren't so visible to others. Discipline is a very complicated, on-going, challenging issue.

Mother-child togetherness is another area that's hard to handle in a group setting, because a child's security is so intangible and hard to explain, and because not pushing a child away takes a mother's energy, too, even if she does feel strongly about her child's need to be with her.

Are you over-sensitive or insecure?
Sometimes mere curiosity ("Do your children *really* sleep with you all night long?") is interpreted as criticism. The best bet is to assume that people are only interested and not criticizing. Your reaction to the questions will be far more confident and less defensive.

If you are insecure, talk to supportive people. Do more reading. *Don't anticipate disagreement with your methods.*

Preventing Criticism
Don't set yourself up for a discussion you don't really want to have. Don't ask what others think if you don't really want to know. When you are with people who do not agree with your discipline methods, and your children are not behaving well, you might say, "I believe in firm discipline and will handle this at home." Then leave immediately, and of course, ask the kids to try a little harder at Aunt Betsy's next time.

When you anticipate disagreement, many times the best recourse is to avoid the issue. For instance, with parents of older children, it does no good to talk about your approach when they have already done things a different way. To belabor the issue will only make them feel guilty. Focus instead on areas where you do have something in common. Be as positive and sincere as you possibly can, and watch that *you* are not being overly critical of *them*.

Remember that the issues which are most tender at this point in your life (such as weaning) won't always be there. Don't ruin a future relationship by focusing on areas of disagreement. This applies to parents, close relatives, friends, and acquaintances.

Offer an explanation of why you do things before you are asked.
This keeps you from being on the defensive and brings the
subject up in order to establish your strong feelings first. One
mother commented, "I have found that very few people will
even attempt to criticize me once they realize I'm beyond
help! And sometimes they see that I have a few valid points."

This whole approach should be made in a gentle way,
letting them know how happy you and the baby are. Janet
Jendron shares from her personal experience:

*When I explain sharing sleep to someone for the first
time, I tell them something like this: "You know, all four
of my children wake up at night. I just can't bear to let
them cry, and I wouldn't get any sleep if I ran all over
the house putting them back to sleep in their own rooms.
So we just sort of have a slumber party in here. It works
best for me at this point in my life." I've never yet had a
person really argue with this. (What are they going to
say, "Yes, you should run all over the house at night and
exhaust yourself"?)*

*Although they sometimes ask questions out of curi-
osity, such as, "Doesn't it get crowded? Aren't you
afraid they'll never want to go back to their own beds?"
I don't view this as criticism, just interest. I would have
had the same natural questions before I had children and
ended up with four wakers. What I tell them may
influence their reaction to the same situation from
someone else in the future.*

It's important that in offering explanations of why you
do things, you give others permission to do things differently. "This works for me and the family in our situation,
but it might not work for you."

Don't flaunt activities that you know will incite controversy.
Plan ahead—breastfeed before visiting an unsupportive
person. Be discreet, if possible, about things like tandem
nursing (nursing two children of different ages) or an older
child nursing. Don't proselytize about sharing sleep. When
you go to visit, let your host put up the crib; don't make
an issue of the fact that you won't use it.

Be careful whom you complain to.
Express your doubts to those who can handle them, like
La Leche League people, close friends, your husband, or
supportive relatives.

> MARTHA: *On the other hand, I've sometimes found
> that admitting doubts to those who don't agree with me
> can make them an ally and create a closer bond. They
> can see that I'm not really a know-it-all, and am just try-
> ing to do my best, like every other mother. When some-
> one feels that you need her emotionally, even a little, she
> is far more accepting of the things you do.*

Coping with Criticism

Rise above criticism and avoid a "holier than thou" attitude.
A positive, non-threatening reply works best. One mother's
reply to the question, "Doesn't it embarrass you to have a
kid that age still nursing?" was "Sometimes it is a little em-
barrassing, but her sweet little nature after she is refueled
makes it worth it." Making light of things often works. For
example, to the question, "You surely don't hold him while
he sleeps!" you could reply, "Yes, isn't it shocking!" To the
statement that, "He'll be nursing when he's in college,"
just smile indulgently and say, "I wouldn't be surprised."

Consider the source.
There are times when it's a waste of effort to get into a discussion. When someone comes in and sighs at your messy
kitchen, you might take it as an attack on your priorities,
which put kids before housework. But there's really no
point in talking about it at the time. We're not out to convert
the world, and won't be able to change everyone's minds
about everything we do. Accept your limitations and relax.

Refer to literature when you think it will help.
Many people are satisfied when they learn that others do the
same things or surveys prove the adequacy of your methods.
However, you'll want to avoid quoting so much that you
get criticized for doing things too much by the book!

Forgiveness is the Key

If you recognize that there really is a lot of stress and pressure from important people in your life because of the way you are parenting your children, especially if there is a lot of bitterness and anger there, some unfinished business probably needs to be taken care of.

Criticism from one's own mother, for example, can be a delicate situation. Feelings run deep between mother and daughter, and there are sometimes unresolved issues. We may expect too much from our mothers, or we may be trying too hard to be "perfect" as we remember they were.

Try to remove yourself a little from the situation and view your mother as a person. Pretend she is a neighbor who just moved in. Very few of us take the time we should to tell our mothers that we appreciate them, that we hold them in esteem as *people*.

One mother had some beautiful thoughts on this:

- First of all, try to be as accepting of your parents as you can. Every time you do something different with your child than they did with you, it's a slap in the face to them. They take it to mean, "I'm raising my baby better than you raised me."
- Try to discuss things calmly and try to put yourself in their place.
- Acknowledge that times and the "experts" change. Admit that in another time and place you might have used a different approach yourself. Tell them you think you turned out pretty well!
- Assure them that your "new and radical" ways are really old ways, tried and true.
- Offer them reading material, but don't be surprised, hurt, or angry if they refuse it.
- Recognize that your mother may be jealous of you. Being a grandmother is a reminder of her own mortality: she may be getting better, but without a doubt she's getting older. She may be envious of your youth, your family situation, your baby, the promise your life holds. This is especially true if

you are breastfeeding successfully and she could not or did not. Your success can be terribly hard on her ego.

Forgiveness is a key issue in the Christian life. When there are hurtful feelings going on between mother and daughter, or between in-laws, it would be wise to seek counseling and have someone pray with you about these issues. There are probably some hurts from the past that need to be forgiven, both of you and from you. Your life as a new parent will be more effective and more honoring to God if you can resolve these hurts and tensions.

Remember that what you perceive as criticism is almost always motivated by love and by a desire to pass on experiences which she feels will help you and your children. It is very, very difficult to step back at some point and simply become friends with adult children. Someday it will be our turn to do just that; we must take care of these points of unfinished business, at least in our own hearts through prayer and forgiveness, so that we do not continue a cycle of hurtful criticism and condemnation.

CHAPTER THIRTEEN

The Payoff

Parents often worry whether they are parenting their children right and how they will turn out. Love for your children makes you vulnerable to those feelings.

We have had the opportunity to study the effects of attachment parenting in thousands of patients over the years, as well as in our own children. While no parents are able to practice all of the attachment styles all of the time, we have observed that children who are reared with the attachment style of parenting still tend to show a number of desirable qualities.

Long-term Effects of Attachment Parenting
Sensitivity. The main quality we notice in attachment-parented babies is sensitivity. Because they grow up in a sensitive and responsive environment, this is the mindset they develop. Because their early care givers were sensitive to their needs, these children are sensitive to others' needs. They are genuinely bothered when another child is hurt. They are concerned about the needs and rights of others.

One of the moral disasters we see in many children is that nothing bothers them. Insensitivity is what gets them into trouble. Many social ills, even wars, can be traced to one group's insensitivity to another.

Attachment-parented children, on the other hand, have a sensitive conscience. They feel right when they do right and wrong when they do wrong. They have a healthy sense of guilt.

Giving. These little takers become big givers because they grow up in a giving environment. Believe it or not, they learn to share more easily—a trait which comes hard to many children. Attachment parents have achieved a balance in their giving, neither indulging nor restraining.

Better disciplined. When children feel right, operate from a basis of trust, and are not angry, they are easier to discipline. Attachment parenting *really* pays off for the high-need baby who, by nature, is at risk for becoming an impulsive child. This unbridled impulsiveness is what gets him into trouble.

High self-esteem. Very early in life this infant received the message, "You have value. You are very important to me." Because the parents spent attachment time with the infant, the child got the message that he was worth spending time with.

Intimacy. These high-touch children become satisfied with people rather than things. They become personally bonded children in a materialistic world. They strive for deep interpersonal relationships. They are not shallow persons.

Spirituality. The real payoff occurs in the child's relationship with God. There is a parallel between the relationship of the child to the parents and the child to God. Because attachment-parented children have early learned the meaning of intimacy with persons, they are more likely to seek intimacy with God. A detached baby is more apt to seek material gratification.

Payoff for the Next Generation

Parents, keep in mind that you are bringing up someone else's future husband or wife, father or mother. The parenting styles which your child learns from you are the ones he is most likely to follow when he becomes a parent. Modeling begins at a very young age.

One day a mother brought in her newborn, Clare, for a check-up, accompanied by her three-year-old daughter, Amanda, the product of attachment parenting.

As soon as Clare started to fuss, Amanda pulled at her mother's skirt saying with much emotion. "Mommy, Clare cry. Pick up, rock-rock, nurse."

Is it hard to guess what Amanda will do someday when her own baby cries? She won't call her doctor. She won't look it up in a book. She will intuitively pick up, rock-rock, and nurse.

Even teenagers pick up on your style of parenting. One day Martha and I were sitting in our family room when we heard our nine-month-old daughter, Erin, crying in our bedroom. As we got near the door, the cries stopped. Curious, we looked in to see why Erin had stopped crying, and what we saw left a warm feeling in our hearts. Jim, our sixteen-year-old athlete, was lying next to Erin, stroking her and gentling her. Why did Jim do this? Because he was following our modeling that when babies cry, someone listens and responds.

Payoff for Parents

Parents reap benefits from attachment parenting, too. The main effect may be summed up in one word: *harmony*. This beautiful term is what attachment parenting is all about. There are various dictionary definitions of harmony, but the simplest and the one we like best is, "Getting along well together."

Attached parents whom we have interviewed make the statements:

> "I feel so connected to my child."

> "I feel right when with him, not right when we are apart."

> "I feel complete."

These are the real bonding effects of attachment parenting.

A feeling we have noticed after practicing this style of parenting with our own children is the deep comfort and peace parents feel when they are truly in tune with their child. Throughout Scripture there is a clear message of the peace and joy humans feel when they are in spiritual harmony. A similar feeling occurs when you are "in sync" with your child. This is clearly stated in Proverbs 29:17, "Discipline your son, and he will give you peace; he will bring delight to your soul." And isn't that, after all, what we're striving for?

BIBLIOGRAPHY

Raising Your Child, Not By Force But By Love
(Sidney D. Craig, The Westminster Press, Philadelphia, PA, 1973).

Childbirth without Fear
(Grantly Dick-Read, M.D., Harper and Row, New York, 1984).

Nurturing Children in the Lord
(Jack Fennema, Ed. D., Presbyterian and Reformed Publishing Co., Phillipsburg, NJ, 1977).

A Shepherd Looks at Psalm 23
(Phillip Keller, Zondervan, Grand Rapids, MI, 1970 [See especially Chapter 8: "Thy Rod and Thy Staff, They Comfort Me."]).

A Good Birth, A Safe Birth
(Diana Korte and Roberta Scaer, Bantam Books, NY, 1984).

Making Your Children Mind Without Losing Yours
(Kevin Lehman, Ph.D., Revell, Old Tappan, NJ, 1983)

Birth Reborn
(Michael Odent, Random House, NY, 1984).

Infant Massage: A Handbook for Loving Parents
(Vimala Schneider McClure, Bantam Books, New York, 1989 [Revised]).

Natural Childbirth and the Christian Family
(Helen Wessel, Bookmates International, Inc./Apple Tree Family Ministries, P.O. Box 9883, Fresno, CA 93794-0883).

Under the Apple Tree: Marrying, Birthing, and Parenting
(Helen Wessel, [Address same as above]).

OTHER BOOKS BY DR. WILLIAM SEARS

The Fussy Baby: How to Bring Out the Best in Your High-Need Child
(New American Library, New York, 1987).

Nighttime Parenting: How to Get Your Baby and Child to Sleep
(New American Library, New York, 1987).

Safe and Healthy: A Parent's Guide to Illnesses and Accidents
(La Leche League International, Franklin Park, IL, 1989).

Becoming A Father: How to Nurture and Enjoy Your Family
(La Leche League International, Franklin Park, IL, 1986).

Growing Together: A Parent's Guide to Baby's First Year
(La Leche League International, Franklin Park, IL, 1987).

Creative Parenting: How to Use the Concept of Attachment Parenting to Raise Children Successfully from Birth to Adolescence
(Dodd, Mead, New York, 1987).

Christian Parenting and Childcare
(Thomas Nelson Publishers, Nashville, TN, 1985)